CH00822206

100 Ideas for Secondary Teachers

Outstanding Geography Lessons

Other titles in the 100 Ideas for Secondary Teachers series:

100 Ideas for Secondary Teachers

Outstanding Geography Lessons

David Rogers

B L O O M S B U R Y
LONDON • OXFORD • NEW YORK • NEW DELHI • SYDNEY

Bloomsbury Education
An imprint of Bloomsbury Publishing Plc

50 Bedford Square, London, WC1B 3DP, UK
1385 Broadway, New York, NY 10018, USA
29 Earlsfort Terrace, Dublin 2, Ireland

www.bloomsbury.com

BLOOMSBURY and the Diana logo are trademarks of Bloomsbury Publishing Plc

First published 2017

Copyright © David Rogers, 2017

David Rogers has asserted his right under the Copyright,
Designs and Patents Act, 1988, to be identified as Author of this work.

All rights reserved. No part of this publication may be reproduced or
transmitted in any form or by any means, electronic or mechanical, including
photocopying, recording, or any information storage or retrieval system,
without prior permission in writing from the publishers.

A catalogue record for this book is available from the British Library.

ISBN
PB: 9781472940995
ePub: 9781472940971
ePDF: 9781472941008

8 10 9 7

Typeset by Newgen Knowledge Works (P) Ltd., Chennai, India
Printed and bound in the UK by CPI Group (UK) Ltd, Croydon CR0 4YY

To find out more about our authors and books visit www.bloomsbury.com.
Here you will find extracts, author interviews, details of forthcoming events
and the option to sign up for our newsletters.

Contents

Acknowledgements

I would like to express my sincere thanks to all of those who have helped shape my career so far. I have been blessed to be able to work with a range of brilliant geography teachers who have provided the atmosphere and stimulus for many of the ideas in this book to germinate, take root and grow.

Many of these ideas were developed during my time at Priory School, so thank you to those who put up with me at Priory Geography. Mo, Jo, Sam, Lisa and Alec: thank you for going along with the crazy plans. We really did change the world.

Thank you to the brilliant geography community: all of those linked to the Royal Geographical Society and Geographical Association. Your commitment and passion for geography never fails to inspire. A hat-tip also to the online geography community, a living testament that teachers who share grow.

Specifically, I'd like to thank the following for contributing to individual ideas through TeachMeets and social media:

Idea 16: Leah Sharp

Idea 24: Noel Jenkins

Idea 37: Daniel Raven Ellison

Idea 55: Ben Crocket

Idea 98: Tony Cassidy

It wouldn't be right for me not to thank Jeff Stanfield. You identified the diamond in the rough and helped nurture my love of helping young people understand the world around them. Many of these activities morphed into what they are now from your ideas.

At times many of the words have tried to wriggle out of my grasp and I would like to thank those who I have burdened with this and helped get them back on the page.

Finally, a massive thank you to the team at Bloomsbury whose encouragement and surgical questions have been invaluable.

Introduction

Great geography teachers change the world. There has never been a more important time for our subject. As the world our students inhabit changes daily, it is up to us to help shape the decision-makers of the future. Geography not only informs us of the world outside of the classroom but enables us to take our part in changing that world.

This book contains the classroom bread and butter that leads to outstanding sequences of lessons. With lesson observations and the outstanding tag currently falling out of fashion, I define 'outstanding' as 'providing high quality learning experiences day in day out'. The ideas are specific to the key concepts of geography whilst also providing some twists on the core activities of every teacher: planning, teaching and feeding back to students.

This book contains a wide range of simple ideas that have been found to have positive impact in geography classrooms, especially when embedded in schemes of learning. I've selected them because as well as helping teachers to deliver outstanding learning experiences, they encourage high quality geographical experiences that will challenge young people.

Many of these ideas aim to save you time, decreasing your workload and enabling you to nudge ever closer to being outstanding.

I used Twitter to ask about what the book should contain, and have entitled the sections according to the main areas requested. This makes the ideas quick and easy to find. I hope that you will be able to weave many of them into your teaching toolkit, and look forward to seeing what you do to adapt, expand and tweak them to fit your context and teaching style. I encourage you to share your experiences of the ideas in this book on Twitter, using the #100Ideas hashtag, or get in touch with me @davidErogers.

As I write this, in Iceland, I am surrounded by the buzz of students who have been enthused by their geography teachers. Never underestimate the influence that you will have on their lives by providing the very best geography learning experiences possible.

Great geography teachers change the world.

David Rogers

How to use this book

This book includes quick, easy and practical ideas for you to dip in and out of, to support you in teaching secondary geography.

Each idea includes:

- A catchy title, easy to refer to and share with your colleagues.
- An interesting quote linked to the idea.
- A summary of the idea in bold, making it easy to flick through the book and identify an idea you want to use at a glance.
- A step-by-step guide to implementing the idea.

Each idea also includes one or more of the following:

Teaching tip	Taking it further	Bonus idea ★
Some extra advice on how or how not to run the activity or put the strategy into practice.	Ideas and advice for how to extend the idea or develop it further.	**There are 17 bonus ideas in this book that are extra exciting and extra original.**

Share how you use these ideas in the classroom and find out what other teachers have done using **#100ideas**.

Sense of place

Part 1

Social data collection

"You actually know some real people, sir?"

Geography lessons require different opinions and a selection of data sources. Bring a real sense of what others think to inform classroom activities by using social media.

Teaching tip

Ensure that you follow your school's social media policy, a copy of which should be available from your IT Department. You don't have to use it in the classroom, just as a data gathering exercise.

As a geographer I love teaching about far-flung places and ideas; however, I'm always wary of presenting an unbalanced point of view. I started asking contacts on Twitter and Facebook some questions and used their answers to generate resources in the classroom. Don't worry if you aren't on social media: gather some information from those in the staffroom, your department or from friends and family.

- Think of a question, for example: 'Do you prefer urban or rural areas and why?' 'What five words spring to mind about national parks?' 'What is your favourite stretch of coastline?' 'What do you think about wind farms?' Keep the question simple.
- Put the question out there. I tend to allow at least two weeks before I want to use the outcome in a lesson.
- Sit back and wait for responses – give a little nudge now and again if needed.
- Convert the responses into data – create a table, graph, word cloud, map or 'talking heads'.
- Get students to respond to the information, whether through data collection, writing or research. For example, when investigating piracy in the Indian Ocean, students could create blog posts and respond to Tweets.

Taking it further

Get your friends to include their postcode in tweets so that students can map locations and investigate spatial patterns using mapping software.

You'll quickly find that giving a real audience to students, their work will improve and they will make the link between the geography of the classroom and real life.

Photo reveal

"A simple idea that stops PowerPoint being pointless."

In such a dynamic subject, the internet ensures that we have access to a wide range of high-quality images to inject interest into our lessons. This idea hides key details of the image, turning them into an effective starter or discussion point.

Choose a digital image and cover key parts of it by using 'shapes' in PowerPoint, then use the 'exit' animation feature to remove them. This encourages classes to think hard about key details and search for evidence. For example:

- A boat marooned on top of a house after Hurricane Katrina – position a rectangle over the bottom part of the image and get students to draw what they expect to see once the bottom part has been revealed.
- Hide a boat in the Aral Sea behind an oblong shape – what is behind the shape?
- Cover an image with ten shapes. Ask students to identify the place by slowly revealing the image. Give more points to those who identify it with fewest clues.
- Once the full image is displayed, get the class to discuss any misconceptions and ideas.

You'll find that your students will begin to really interrogate and think about the image, and this prepares them with the skills they will need for examinations in which they have to identify key features of an area and make assumptions using the evidence.

Taking it further

Combine this idea with Idea 37 'Beat the teacher'.

Bonus idea ★

This idea can be adapted in many ways, e.g. ask students to draw what they would expect to see or write a descriptive paragraph containing good geographical terms. Students' sense of place will quickly develop, although don't overdo this activity as your classes will always be looking for the catch!

Geography is enquiry

"Now every lesson is an enquiry, we can apply our ideas to the real world with ease."

The enquiry process is central to geography and it's vital that students become familiar with it early on. This tried and tested idea, when used right from lesson one of Year 7, introduces the process straight away and helps to develop independence.

Teaching tip

Transform the enquiry process into a flow chart and create A3 laminated table mats. Children can refer to these during lessons.

On the wall of every classroom place the following rules of enquiry:

1. Ask questions – quality questions take time to develop.
2. Gather information – geographers need to collect information from a range of reliable sources.
3. Evaluate that information – does the information show bias? Are different points of view represented?
4. Present findings and conclusions – consider presentations, blogs and videos as well as written reports.
5. Evaluate your enquiry – the most important part! Remember that there should be a self-evaluation as well as teacher feedback.

Develop every lesson using these skills. From Year 7 onwards, get students to be nosy by asking great geographical questions. Teach them to evaluate everything (from textbooks to web pages, and even the teacher's viewpoint) and select an appropriate technique to share the information.

Over time, classes will become more independent as they frame their ideas using the enquiry process. Remember that enquiry is to geography what the scientific method is to science.

Monster mouth

"Now I understand how to use Google Earth to allow a class to relate to a faraway place."

A major problem for students is putting places into context. Geography is full of dazzling facts and figures; however, these can be difficult to interpret unless we connect the faraway place with something more familiar.

I love using multi-use case studies. For example, when investigating the Amazon rainforest, it makes sense to study the Amazon River. The trouble is, unless we actually go there, the scale of the river is difficult to understand. I first used Google Earth to help students get their heads around the size of the Amazon River, as in the example below, but then quickly adapted it to other places.

- Get students to describe the mouth of the Amazon River.
- Display your school on Google Earth and then fly from your school to the mouth of the Amazon. This helps students get a sense of direction and distance.
- Use the distance-measuring tool to measure the river's width. Write this down.
- Next, visit a location closer to home and do the same. For example, I teach on the South Coast so I use the width of the English Channel.

Using this technique, classes will be able to gain a better understanding of the scale of different locations.

Teaching tip

Create KML placemarks for different locations as this makes it quicker to move between areas. KML placemarks contain simple information about places in Google Earth. You can find tutorials on how to create them by searching on YouTube.

Taking it further

Deciding how to measure the river is a good discussion point, and switching between the different units of measurement available in Google Earth provides the opportunity to develop numeracy skills.

Curiosity kits

"I never knew you had a life outside this classroom, Mr Rogers!"

Bring your own experiences in to the classroom and introduce a new place or topic by showing the class artefacts from that place. Get them to guess where you've been to acquire these objects.

Teaching tip

This technique is great for developing literacy and descriptions of places so ask the class to record key words and write a 'so that' sentence for each object.

Geography teachers are generally a well-travelled bunch and we benefit from the fact that the content of our subject is outside of the classroom, meaning that we have direct experience of its many aspects. I managed to procure an old-fashioned, battered suitcase from a charity shop and turned this into my curiosity kit.

- Fill the suitcase with a selection of objects that link to your chosen topic, e.g. walking equipment for a National Park; comfortable shoes and a shopping bag for retail; pumice, ash and volcanic rock for Iceland.
- Slowly reveal each item to the class. Allow them to examine each object in turn and provide a focus by asking them to try to describe the place they think the artefacts represent, and why those items have been chosen.

The most important part of this activity is to follow up with geographical writing. Ask the class to write a geographical description of the place, using key geographical words. Give students a list of these words and allow them access to an atlas or other map so that they can locate the place.

Image of the day

"Geography really is everything, Miss!"

Getting students to look deeply in to an image is important. This method also shows that geography really is all around us and uses a freely available resource to generate discussion and consolidate knowledge.

I can be a pretty predictable teacher sometimes, and I often use the Bing.com search homepage (this is the page displayed when you visit Bing.com) to start lessons or to consolidate knowledge. It's also great to use for the occasional test. Basically, Bing uses a different image every day. These are random and brings home the point that geography is *everything*.

Teaching tip

If you're less confident being at the whim of a random image, screenshot a selection of images and save them for later use.

Display the homepage and ask the class to consider an appropriate question:

- Can you identify primary, secondary, tertiary and quaternary economic activities?
- Is this landscape produced by weather or climate?
- Can you explain how this landscape was formed?
- Is this erosion or weathering?
- Can you identify human activities and land uses?
- How does this image link to our topic?

Bing also links to topical events and occasionally provides a brief video as a backdrop. This method can save on planning and can be used at the end of lessons when you need to refocus the class. I often drop this activity in to revise topics ahead of mock examination time.

Bonus idea ★

Ask a member of your tutor group to select an image of the week. Display it on your classroom wall along with a simple question.

360° video

"I was able to get a real sense of what the place is like."

The geography classroom is home to learning about far-flung places and unfamiliar environments. Using 360 degree images and video allows students to gain a more detailed insight into some of the world's greatest locations.

Teaching tip

Purchasing a cheap VR viewer means that young people can explore locations in an immersive way. They're especially useful for introducing different environments.

Taking it further

If possible, purchase or rent a 360 degree camera for your department and capture images of key fieldwork locations. This will allow classes to become familiar with the location before they visit, as well as providing a useful reference point once back in the classroom.

YouTube videos and images are common implements of the geography teachers toolkit. These days, videos and images provide 360 degree panoramas of locations. These excellent resources inject interest and drama. For example, check out Mammut's projects:

- 360 degree video of climbing the north face of the Eiger: http://bit.ly/2aNDUi4
- 360 degree image of Everest Base Camp: http://bit.ly/2b2sSCV

These can be used to:

- identify glacial features
- write a detailed description of the location
- note human impact on the location.

Head over to YouTube and with a little searching you can find 360 degree videos of beaches, river features and rainforest locations. Indeed, most faraway places can be effectively introduced by using freely available 360 degree videos.

Twitter feedback

"I enjoyed getting feedback from real people so that I could improve my work."

Often, students only benefit from feedback from their teacher. Putting their work on Twitter provides a wider audience for their work, invites comments from further afield, and can be used to present further challenge to the class.

Assuming that your school allows mobile devices in the classroom, take photographs of great work and attach them to a tweet. Wait a while, and over time your network will start to provide feedback to the student, providing them with a list of comments for a subsequent lesson. You'll find that most students will love their work being published on the internet (just ensure no names are visible on the work). Giving a real purpose to their work also improves engagement.

Furthermore, once the images are on Twitter, it's possible to show them to the class via a projector – a simple way to model work without a visualiser.

Teaching tip

This technique can also be used to quickly display great work or work that you want to discuss as you can easily display it via your Twitter profile, projected on the whiteboard.

Taking it further

Get students to publish their work in a blog and get feedback from their peers.

How many UKs can you get in...?

"Maths and problem-solving skills are well developed in geography lessons."

Effective maths skills are vital in geography. Encourage problem-solving and estimation skills by challenging the class to calculate how many times the UK would fit into the place under investigation.

I try to ensure that maths skills are well developed across geography, especially as students need to be able to get to grips with complex data sets. The bonus of this idea is that students also develop their sense of scale for the place under investigation. It seems that many places are compared with the size of Wales, so this develops upon that idea.

The land area of the United Kingdom is 248,531.52km^2 (source: http://bit.ly/2eVkzKX). When introducing a new place, whether it be the continent of Africa, Antarctica or the Brazilian rainforest, I get the class to calculate how many times the UK fits into that country. Make it more interesting by banning calculators!

Teaching tip

It's worth checking in with your maths department to find out how students calculate estimations, as this will allow you to reinforce these skills.

Taking it further

This idea can be adapted to different scales by finding out the land area of your settlement, county or region. For example, how many times does Brighton fit into the Vatnajökull icecap in Iceland?

Map madness

"I like that this idea can be used in an exam answer when I'm under pressure."

Spatial awareness is vital in geography, as is a good working knowledge of places, especially under the new national curriculum. Getting a class to create sketch maps from memory strengthens their locational knowledge and improves their notes — it also saves on the photocopying bill!

Under pressure to cut down the photocopying bill and frustrated at the poor locational knowledge of the UK demonstrated by my Year 10 class, I challenged them to create a sketch map of the country using four triangles. They then had to add the approximate location of the four capital cities and our own location. The triangles could be any type and in any orientation. Once done, I asked individuals to share their efforts using the visualiser.

This was initially used to allow them to create quick sketch maps in their notebooks, where further detail could be added, such as:

- details of the air masses that affect the UK
- the location of major transport routes and major industry
- the sequence of weather in a depression or anticyclone.

Not only did I find that the quality of their notes improved, but so did their locational knowledge.

Taking it further

Challenge classes to create world maps or deconstruct Europe into a series of geometrical shapes.

Dotocracy

"Having a limited number of dots really made me consider carefully which was the best answer."

This simple peer assessment technique has many applications, from selecting the best work to voting on a particular fieldwork technique. Try it during a decision-making exercise to help develop students' reasoning skills.

Teaching tip

Use examples of real work from mock examination answers as this provides a real context for where the mistakes can be made.

When providing feedback on a class's examination performance, use a range of model answers to develop their understanding of how to apply what they know in the exam. It's really important that students know where they can improve, so select a number of example answers that are very close to each other: it's easy to spot a full mark answer from a middle answer.

Provide a set of sticky dots to each student – I find giving three each is a good number. The next part is simple; each individual must distribute their stickers by attaching them to the answer that they think is best. If they aren't sure, they can split their dots, perhaps attaching only one to three different answers.

By running this activity in groups or as a whole class, I'm able to explore some of the reasons why an answer is the best, e.g. it has great geographical terminology, or because it provides both negative and positive aspects.

This can also be used to:

- select the most appropriate graph type for a data set
- select the best data collection techniques ahead of a fieldwork investigation.

Mind the gap!

"I hadn't considered exploring development indicators in that way."

Gapminder.org is a brilliant visualisation tool that can be used to reinforce students' understanding of the relationship between development indicators and strengthen their understanding of mathematical relationships.

Many geography teachers miss the opportunity to develop a deep understanding of the relationship between development indicators. The Gapminder World visualisation is an accessible yet powerful tool for displaying the relationships between different development factors.

Teaching tip

Gapminder World provides an ideal opportunity to reinforce the idea of positive and negative correlations.

- Display the Gapminder World visualisation: head to www.gapminder.org and then select 'Gapminder World' from the top menu. The default shows GDP per capita against life expectancy. Here the relationship is that as a country gets richer, people live longer.
- Keep the x axis as GDP and select another variable on the y axis using the drop-down menu. For example fertility, literacy rate or CO_2 emissions. There are many variables available, so do set aside some time to explore!
- Before displaying the graph, ask students to write their prediction of the relationship. For example, 'I predict that fertility rate will decrease in richer countries, which is a negative correlation.' Be prepared to model this for the first attempt.
- Display the actual relationship and explore the possible reasons for it.

I've found this very useful for dispelling students' misconceptions about development. For example, there isn't a clear relationship between military spending and GDP.

Predicting the graph

"My GCSE students understand the changes of the demographic transition model much better now."

Interrogating graphs is an important skill for geographers to develop. To increase the challenge, however, try presenting students with the labelled axes without the completed graph and ask them to predict the result.

Make this activity less challenging by providing additional details to begin with, such as specific key dates and data points. This means that the students can decide whether the rate of change was constant or changed at a particular point in time.

This simple idea generates great discussion around the relationship between different variables. Start by providing a blank graph with the x and y axes labelled, e.g.

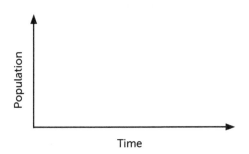

Next, challenge the class to predict the pattern of population growth in a certain time frame. Use this to generate discussion around the graph before revealing the actual graph and allowing individuals to compare their predictions with the actual data. This idea can be used in a number of topics such as:

- net migration
- the demographic transition model
- the proportion of economic activities in the UK over time
- how discharge may respond to a rainfall event on a flood hydrograph.

Once completed, ask the class to add on additional detail, e.g. the Industrial Revolution.

Getting the travel bug

"Using geocaching generates a real enthusiasm for geography and different places."

Geocaching is a treasure hunt game that spans the globe with millions of 'caches' to be found. By creating a trackable 'travel bug' with a mission, students can track its progress and use the data to create investigations and practise maths skills.

'Travel bugs' are physical tokens that are found cheaply on the internet and, when registered at geocaching.com, it's possible to track their movements online via a map and accompanying statistics.

This idea first came about in the build-up to the London 2012 Olympics when my Year 8 class wanted to get a travel bug to travel to Rio by 2016. The online map is used to track the rate of progress and the statistics can be used to calculate the average distance travelled per day.

Once you've purchased a few, simply create a geocaching account and follow the simple instructions to set them free in the wild! Do this by placing your travel bug in a local geochache. They move around the world as other people discover your bug's mission, pick it up and then deposit it in another cache they visit in the future. Using travelbugs is less fiddly than creating your own cache, as you can start the journey by placing them in existing caches. This idea is great for conveying a sense of scale to students and also gives them a context within which to investigate the different places that are visited.

Teaching tip

This is an idea that requires a bit of planning. Head over to geocaching. com and watch this YouTube video, https:// youtu.be/Tdh-KYwAGsk, to get a basic overview of what geocaching is. I'd recommend that you download the free app and go geocaching yourself: there are millions across the world and the liklihood is that there will be a number local to your school or home. Armed with this basic knowledge, you'll easily be able to follow this idea.

Taking it further

Create a map display to keep track of your travel bugs and their progress, or use an overseas trip to set one free in a different country.

Rich to poor: mystery countries

"Using this method over and over developed my students' understanding of development data."

Geographers need to be able to assess data sets quickly and then process the information. By providing different data sets and asking the class to rank the countries in order of wealth, they have to understand the data presented.

Teaching tip

Ensure you add in some red herrings that don't really help identify whether a country is rich or poor, e.g. military spending.

I like to give similar activities time and again as this reinforces the key learning and ensures that students access the knowledge required over and over again, helping them to remember.

Display four or five development indicators for four to eight different countries. Hide the country name and choose a selection of social and economic indicators. Try to avoid the obvious ones, such as GDP, where the answer is straightforward. Great examples to use are:

- fertility rate
- literacy rate
- life expectancy
- economic structure profile
- population age profile
- number of doctors
- energy consumption
- calories consumed.

Give the class five minutes in which to rank the countries from most developed to least developed. This reinforces the importance of data and allows the class to practise their understanding of how each development indicator works. The name of the country isn't that important, but they should be able to classify them, e.g. which are advanced or emerging economies, least developed etc.

Taking it further

Use this technique as a revision tool by asking the class to define each development indicator in the grid.

Show me the numbers

"Make it easy to understand big numbers visually."

There are a lot of very big numbers in geography. Often, students won't comprehend the size and scale of their own settlement, never mind be able to meaningfully compare it with another. Get them to create 3D models that display the numbers visually, however, and they are more likely to get the link.

When comparing two urban areas such as Brighton and London, it's quite often difficult to get across the differences in scale in land area and population. Provide the class with:

- some Lego™ bricks and mini whiteboards, or other suitable materials
- comparative data for a range of information, e.g. total population, land area, economic structure, number and type of services.

Next, ask them to construct a scale based upon the information, e.g. each Lego™ brick could represent 100 people and each mini whiteboard 10 square miles. Once this is done, groups can construct models that visually depict the differences. From this, construct a visual settlement hierarchy with different settlement types, using local information where possible.

Finally, and most importantly, get the class to write their comparisons using the information gleaned from the activity. Insist that they include facts and figures as well as comparative terms.

Teaching tip

It's always better for students to carry out mathematical processes rather than include raw numbers so get them to work out *how* much bigger one settlement is than another.

Taking it further

Photograph the creations and make a display with them. You could even include settlements from other countries.

Map battle!

"There is life beyond the Ordnance Survey."

Ordnance Survey mapping is the best in the world and is the bedrock of many other mapping applications such as satellite navigation and geographical information systems. However, there are many other types of map. This activity allows students to identify the most important features of effective maps.

Taking it further

After this activity, challenge the class to produce a map of the school tailored to different users. How would it differ from other maps of the location?

I am a map geek. I have many maps and always grab a paper map when I'm travelling. Go beyond the Ordnance Survey by letting students explore a large range of maps, e.g.

- Icelandic road atlas
- Olympic park map
- Wipe-clean map of the world showing the continents.
- Tube map
- Map of the Hundred Acre Wood
- A Harveys map for a mountain marathon
- A school map for new students
- A shopping centre map
- The map on a tourist attraction leaflet
- Google Maps.

Ask pupils to compare the different maps and compile a table to analyse the features, e.g.

- What is each map for? (Purpose)
- Who is each map for?
- What special features does it have?
- What is the scale?
- Which is the best map? Why?
- What special features would you include in your map?

Using a lesson or two to explore maps instead of teaching basic map skills deepens students' understanding of the key features of maps and how they meet the needs of their users.

Bonus idea ★

If you have any input in the homework planner for your institution make sure a world map gets added. If this isn't possible, get one stuck into each exercise book. Referring to it often will improve students' knowledge of where places are.

Literacy

Part 2

Banned words

"This really helped me to improve my grades!"

Literacy is everything, and often students lose critical marks because of using the wrong word. The whole aim of this approach is that, when used from day one of Year 7, students become used to writing succinct answers that use specific geographical terminology.

Teaching tip

I recommend embedding this technique throughout your teaching, right from the first lesson in Year 7.

Taking it further

It's also possible to enhance this method by developing a 'heavenly word ceiling': put some good examples of words and phrases on the ceiling.

Bonus idea ★

Combine this technique with 'think, pair, write, share' (see Idea 93) or give out example answers with banned words in them.

Banned words is a very simple idea that has a huge impact. Be careful though, as your students will be picking you up on your words! This idea first came to me when I was trying to improve the quality of students' written responses. The problem was that they weren't using specific geographical terminology.

The first step is to create a 'banned words' board somewhere prominent in your classroom. Add the following words:

- stuff
- things
- people
- pollution
- affect
- up, right, left, down
- impossible.

Then refer to the words all the time. You really can't overdo it! Some of the words are 'semi-banned.' This means that they have to be qualified, e.g. 'air pollution' or 'negatively affected.'

Don't even let the students use these words in verbal responses and you'll soon see the quality of their work improve.

Bipolar adjectives

"Improve comparisons!"

Being able to compare two or more locations is a useful skill for geographers. Bipolar adjectives provide a scaffold upon which to build extended writing during follow-up work, as well as developing students' geographical terminology.

When investigating migration, my class always look at the differences between migration into the USA from Mexico and Canada. Google Earth allows us to look closely at borders from above and through street view, and there are a number of programs that also provide visual ideas of the border. However, I found that the writing produced after examining these was lacking in development, so I used paired adjectives to support the writing.

Paired adjectives provide students with a bipolar scale on which to judge two, or more, different places. Provide as many sets of adjectives as you need and ask the students to make a judgement whilst looking at the resources for each place.

- Scary   1   5   10   Safe
- Protected   1   5   10   Unprotected
- Flat   1   5   10   Steep
- Rural   1   5   10   Urban
- Rich   1   5   10   Poor
- Full   1   5   10   Empty
- Attractive   1   5   10   Ugly
- Interesting 1   5   10   Boring

This idea improves the confidence of those with low levels of literacy, as they will have a range of adjectives readily available. You can increase your expectations by allowing students to add their own adjectives.

Teaching tip

It's useful to provide a space for students to record their own adjectives and any facts or figures that they want to include that link to the adjectives.

Taking it further

Provide a selection of data and statistics for each place, e.g. number of border crossings, and encourage individuals to weave this in to their writing by linking to the appropriate adjective.

V.C.O.G

"See the extended writing of low attainers really develop!"

Being able to produce extended pieces of persuasive writing is essential for successful geographers. This is an idea from a literacy lead I used to work with that I adapted for geography.

Teaching tip

The V.C.O.G grid could be displayed on the board but by providing printed copies you can also differentiate them to the individual needs of students therefore providing both stretch and support.

V.C.O.G stands for:

- **V**ocabulary – provide the key words and terms that you'd expect to see in a quality answer. Challenge students to use them all, or a proportion of them to add differentiation.
- **C**onnectives – the key to extended writing is to expand on all points as much as possible, reinforce this by providing a range of connectives.
- **O**peners – often getting started is the problem. Provide as many sentence starters as you need.
- **G**roups of people – students often forget to write about key groups of people so include a list of who should be considered.

It's essentially a method of scaffolding students' writing as they practise extended writing. Simply, divide a PowerPoint slide into four (one for each of V.C.O.G) and provide a range of helpful phrases for each section. I use this to support an end of unit assessment of a decision-making write up. For example:

Key question: Describe the challenges of living in a shanty town.

- Vocabulary: MEDC, LEDC, rural, urban, physical features, human features, climate, quality of life, life expectancy, $GDP per capita, sanitation, medical/healthcare, infrastructure.
- Connectives: however, likewise, whereas, even though, on the other hand, unlike, contrasting to, in addition to, despite, because, so as to, nevertheless, although, similarly.

- Openers: The biggest problem facing this shanty town is . . . Residents are affected by . . .
- Groups of people: residents of the shanty town, the city council, wealthy residents living nearby.

By using V.C.O.G sheets in every lesson you'll find your students' confidence develops quickly along with their use of geographical terms. The idea can also be adapted for use with GCSE case study and decision-making exercises. After teaching the content and asking the class to decide upon their decision, simply introduce the V.C.O.G sheet adapted to the question. Over time, it's possible to reduce the level of support so that the students are producing high-quality examination answers, especially when combined with 'banned words' (see Idea 18). For example:

Key question: How sustainable is tourism in Iceland?

- Vocabulary: MEDC, LEDC, rural, urban, physical features, human features, climate, sustainability, social, economic, environmental, resident, tourist, government.
- Connectives: however, likewise, whereas, even though, on the other hand, unlike, contrasting to. in addition to, despite, because, so as to, nevertheless, although, similarly.
- Openers: Tourism in Iceland can be considered . . . Sustainability means that . . . In order to be sustainable, Iceland's tourism must . . . The social impacts of the volcanic eruption were . . . however . . . The volcanic eruption caused . . . however, this is sustainable because . . .
- Groups: Icelandic government, school leavers, Gatwick airport, farmers, tour operators.

Students respond better when there is a question to answer as this develops the enquiry process, so ensure that's at the top of the page. You could save a bank of V.C.O.G resources as PowerPoint files which are quick to adapt for any situation.

Taking it further

Provide blank V.C.O.G grids to a GCSE group to help them plan essay answers to case study or decision-making questions.

Bill Shakespeare was a geographer

"I noticed that students' understanding of how places affect people deepened when I introduced fictional writing into lessons."

Geographers are never off-duty! Next time you're reading a book, highlight passages and use them in lessons. Not only will this technique model great writing, it will fire up the interest and imagination of your students.

Teaching tip

Talking about the books you read is important in modelling to young people that reading is not only useful, but enjoyable. Develop a display that shares what you are currently reading to students and set up a bookshelf where you can keep past reads, or a selection of books from the library. This provides a great talking point and models how important reading is to geographers and that geography is a major part of pretty much everything.

When I worked with Jeff Stanfield, former geography advisor in Hampshire, he used to often mention the fact that many fictional and non-fictional writers are very good at describing people and places.

The beauty of this is that, as you read books, which let's face it is usually during the summer holidays, it's easy to build up a collection of suitable passages about different geographical landscapes and contexts, e.g.

- Chris Hadfield describing the landscape and climate of the Russian steppe as a landing zone for the Soyuz capsule in *An astronaut's guide to life on Earth*.
- Gregory Roberts exploring the slum landscape of Mumbai *Shantaram*.
- Michael Ridpath portraying the Icelandic landscape in the *Fire and Ice* detective series.
- Joe Simpson describing the glacial landscape in *Touching the Void*.

There are a number of ways in which passages can be used:

- Provide each student with a copy of the passage with key geographical words and phrases blanked out – can they add these in?
- Read to the class – even hardened Year 11s enjoy being read to and this can provide good context before looking at the detail of a case study.

Silent weather forecasts

"Develop succinct, precise geographical writing."

It's one thing to develop good geographical writing, but accurate and quality explanation and description needs to extend to verbal communication also. Use a freely available weather forecast to develop quality speech and writing and allow students to practise their knowledge of weather patterns. The trick? Mute the sound.

Use the short summary forecast found on the BBC's weather pages; this is updated a few times each day and is therefore a useful way of comparing the predictions with what happens in real life. Using silent weather forecasts provides an opportunity to develop pupils' ability to talk and write about the weather, and the BBC presenters are masters of combining description with explanation.

I usually show the forecast three or four times to the class, each time focusing on a different aspect:

- What information is provided to the viewer? Which geographical terms will be needed?
- How is data used in the forecast? Do we need the spoken words?
- Which aspects may need explaining?
- What potential impacts should viewers be warned about?

Next, I get the students to write their forecast and allow them to practise the delivery. For fun, it's always good to get a few 'volunteers' to read theirs out over the muted forecast, before playing the forecast with the sound turned up.

Throw in this exercise several times over the course of a term in order to revisit and practise this skill.

Teaching tip

It's best to cover weather and climate in the autumn or spring term when Atlantic depressions are likely to be affecting Britain's weather. It's so much easier teaching about the sequence of a depression when it's actually happening. Decide when to teach certain subjects to make the most of natural events, e.g. teaching about hurricanes during September when it's likely that there will be one in the Atlantic. This reinforces the links between the geography classroom and the real world.

'So what?' and 'prove it!'

"When I see 'So what?' on my work or Sir says, 'Prove it!' it's annoying, but I know that it improves my writing so I'll get a better grade."

Good quality geographical writing needs two key aspects: data to support the writer's claims, and fully developed explanations. By using 'So what?' and 'Prove it!' often, students soon get the message.

Taking it further

Use this technique when marking books and you'll soon be saving time. I use the symbol ∧ for so what? and ! for prove it. In the following lesson, get students to respond to these symbols by improving their work.

I find that simple phrases and mantras, used often, rapidly improve young people's writing. In my classroom I have two key phrases which are up on the walls and which I use in my marking and in my responses to verbal answers:

- 'So what?' – This means that the student has provided a cracking piece of information and made a fantastic geographical point, but needs to expand on it further, e.g. 'Poor sanitation means that local residents would become ill' turns into 'Poor sanitation means that local residents would become ill, which means that they may be unable to work. In turn this could cause stress for the family and mean that they are unable to meet the cost of basic necessities such as food and rent.'
- 'Prove it!' – A strong piece of writing is often let down by a lack of factual information that supports the arguments put forward. Use this to encourage the class to develop the habit of using evidence as a matter of routine.

One word each

"This really makes you think quickly and listen to the rest of the class."

Sometimes I want to involve every student and end the lesson by summarising the learning whilst using key geographical terms. By limiting each student in the room to one word as they construct sentences with their peers, it is possible to check understanding and get everyone involved.

'One word each' can be used at the beginning of a lesson to recap prior learning, or at the end to summarise the key points of a lesson. Get the class into small groups and choose a range of key terms that need to be included, e.g.

- gravity
- abrasion
- fault.

You may also wish to provide some connectives to the class or individuals.

Explain that each member of the group can only say one word, then the sentence is continued by the next member of the group. Present the question (e.g. "Describe the formation of a sea stack") and give a minute or so of thinking time. This is best done if nothing is written down, as students have to retain the information in their working memory. The important rule is that, when put together, their explanation makes sense and is coherent.

Next, allow each group to take turns to give their explanation, with each individual only permitted to utter one word at a time. This activity generates much energy and, most importantly, develops listening and communication skills as well as polishing the use of geographical terms.

Teaching tip

This technique takes a bit of practice and perseverance, from both yourself and your classes. Don't be afraid to stop the activity if poor quality words start to slip in.

Taking it further

Try removing the lists of connectives and key geographical terms for more challenge, or for a real challenge involve the whole class and remove the planning time!

Transform knowledge into animation

"I found that I was able to recall specific information long after I'd completed this activity in class."

Improve the retention of case study knowledge by transforming it into animation using hand-held devices. These have the added benefit of creating revision resources that can be hosted online.

Teaching tip

Speak nicely to your science technicians as you'll find that clamp stands are excellent substitutes for video tripods!

I was becoming increasingly frustrated with one Year 10 class' inability to write high-quality case study answers. At the time, mobile devices with recording and editing capabilities were becoming commonplace, and I stumbled upon a blog post by Noel Jenkins explaining how RSA-style animations can be used to summarise data.

The plan is simple: once students are familiar with the basic video and editing capabilities of their device, simply rig up a tripod and get students to draw out their learning. The basic idea is that the students turn their knowledge into a drawing: they film themselves drawing and then use the video editing software afterwards to add narration. You can read a full account here: http://bit.ly/2eRUI71. The result can be sped up narration added in time with the animation. The activity requires planning, careful drafting of scripts and the inclusion of place-specific detail.

I found that when followed up with case study questions, the students' performance improved, even when revisited many months later. Furthermore, by hosting the results on YouTube, we built up a bank of revision resources.

See an example here: http://bit.ly/2aSZjnY

Make it 140!

"Brilliant for differentiation and helping pupils remember key information."

Students often struggle with remembering key facts and information about a case study. In this activity they are challenged to summarise and simplify a complex set of information into 140 characters or less.

If, like me, you have a small child, you'll have read many picture books. One series in particular combined a complicated story, a simplified summary and an image on each page. This meant that that the book challenged my son at different stages of learning how to read. I adapted this idea for the classroom.

Divide an A4 page into three: start by including an image related to the case study and a long piece of text. I tend to use a model, full mark GCSE answer here, but you could use an extract from a news website or textbook. Ask the students to simplify and summarise the text into no more than 140 characters. This may seem a challenge at first, but it allows students to pick out the main points of the text.

This technique can be adapted by providing the simplified text and image and challenging the class to produce a model answer from the information given.

Teaching tip

By using PowerPoint to create each page, the process can be modelled to classes. First reveal the image and engage the class with it, then the long text.

Taking it further

Combine this with Idea 1 and provide an image and a tweet that students then use as the basis for an investigation – expanding on the tweet's information.

'This means that...'

"Improve the quality of explanation."

Often, students are able to remember and produce the bare facts in an examination question well. The 'This means that......' technique challenges them to expand on each point as much as possible.

Teaching tip

Get the students to produce the basic facts for homework and then expand on them in the lesson.

I thought I was doing really well with my students being able to remember and classify the types of coastal defence, reel off the causes of desertification, or list with gusto the problems of living in a rural community without services in the UK. However, I was brought back down to earth when I realised that the same individuals were unable to expand on their points when it came to the big six-mark questions that demanded developed explanations.

To combat this, I began providing the students with the basic points and asking them to expand them in class instead by using the connective 'this means that', e.g.

- Overgrazing – this means that...
- Collecting firewood – this means that...
- A sea wall is hard engineering – this means that....
- Elderly residents are without easy transport – this means that...

Taking it further

Model this technique during questioning, always insisting that a basic point is followed up with a 'this means that' explanation.

Follow up the exercise with some sample questions and you should find that the quality of explanations quickly improves.

Fieldwork

Part 3

Film yourself drawing diagrams

"I came across this idea at a TeachMeet and put it into action the very next day."

Being able to produce accurate diagrams is a key geographical skill and should be modelled by the teacher. Encourage students to practise at home by filming yourself drawing key diagrams.

Teaching tip

Encourage students to number their annotations on diagrams to show the chronological nature of the process being depicted e.g. relief rainfall.

Taking it further

This technique can also be used to demonstrate how to annotate photographs and maps.

Bonus idea ★

Embed your masterpiece on a PowerPoint slide then play on a loop as students construct their own copy.

Think for a moment about how many diagrams students have to produce in geography. Types of rainfall, longshore drift, waterfalls and oxbow lakes are amongst the most common. Often, especially with lower attaining students, although they may remember the diagram they may forget how to construct it, especially under exam conditions.

Of course, in usual circumstances teachers will draw each diagram on the board as the class follows along, adding key annotations as they go. It's easy to improve the support given, however, by filming yourself drawing the diagrams. Don't panic: it's not necessary to appear in the video, but you may wish to ensure your fingernails are clean! Simply set up a filming device above a blank sheet of paper, select your drawing implement of choice, hit record and draw. See an example at the end of this video: http://bit.ly/2auqxVt.

I tend to use a mobile device that allows me to upload the video straight onto YouTube, making it accessible to all of my students.

Land use over the fence

"It's amazing that there are discernible land use patterns around our school."

Getting off-site can be a mission. Instead, get classes to peer over the school fence to record land use patterns and practise key data collection techniques.

Time off-site is valuable when teaching students the techniques required to collect primary evidence. By taking advantage of the area around your school, your students can learn these essential methods without time consuming and costly off-site arrangements.

- Start by defining a clear geographical question. Ours was: 'Does the surrounding area display the characteristics of the rural-urban fringe?'
- Provide some OS maps at different scales along with satellite imagery and ask the class to predict what they will see. With lower year groups this is a great reinforcement of map skills and compass directions.
- Students will also develop their map interpretation skills, and you'll find it illuminates which features and characteristics they miss despite passing the area every day. Following the geographical enquiry model, what do the students expect to see?
- Next, collect information. I found that we could successfully collect useful information such as pedestrian and traffic counts, and land use surveys, as well as creating annotated field sketches and photographs.
- The class then present and analyse the data they have collected before providing a conclusion.

After conducting this, I found that students wasted less time when we could get them off-site and straight into the data collection. In addition, they are able to practise and hone their analysis and presentation skills.

Teaching tip

Don't assume anything! Plan to teach explicitly the skills around data presentation and analysis. Ensure you give enough time to run through the basics of data presentation, including which graph to use and how to include accurate axis labels and titles.

Taking it further

Once the techniques have been taught, get students to practise them on their way home by creating a transect of their route to school.

Sensory microclimate

"Improve your students' understanding of primary data collection."

Challenge classes to gather scientific information and complete a fieldwork enquiry on the grounds of your school.

Teaching tip

It's well worth experimenting with making your own equipment first. A quick search on YouTube will yield some great examples.

Using very little apart from a handful of thermometers and an anemometer, this is an excellent activity if you are frustrated with the lack of fieldwork equipment available in your school. I wanted Year 7 to collect robust data and conduct an on-site fieldwork enquiry around the hypothesis: 'Our school has no impact on its microclimate.'

This is very obvious to solve even if students only have a basic knowledge of climate. Remember that students should get into the habit of providing evidence that supports their ideas and findings. The lesson sequence goes like this:

- Start on a small scale. Leave some thermometers out around a school building, ensuring to cover all aspects (north, south, east and west). Visit each location, recording the temperature and wind speed and making a note of variables, such as shade. This gives students the opportunity to scientifically measure the difference in temperature, whilst theorising about what causes those differences.
- Next, scale the enquiry up to cover the whole school ... but, and this is the twist, ban them from using any scientific equipment. For homework, challenge individuals to devise a way of measuring the variables and recording the outcome.
- Allocate a lesson for the class to conduct their measurements and follow up with the usual data presentation and conclusions.

I found that Year 7 students are ingenious and the project allowed us to teach about sampling, recording numerical information and being able to prove a hypothesis.

Photo orienteering

"It's great fun getting to know our new school and at the same time practising our map skills."

Combine photo interpretation with map skills by getting students out of the classroom and locating places in and around the school by stating their grid reference.

It's important to leave the classroom when teaching map skills. This activity came about because we wanted to assess the map skills of a new intake whilst helping to make them feel more at home around the school.

- Take up to 20 photos in and around the school. If you're evil-minded like me, you'll make some really obscure. Make sure you take images of small details rather than obvious locations, e.g. a distinctive sign.
- Pair up your class, providing each pair with a set of numbered images and a map of the school. Consider giving either a laminated satellite image or an OS MasterMap scale with a grid system superimposed.
- Each pair has to explore the school, locating each image and recording the six-figure grid reference.

Teaching tip

OS MasterMaps are available with a subscription to Digimap, and are essential for every geography department.

Taking it further

Superimpose a map of the world over the base map and ask students to name the country or continent each place is located in, as well as the grid reference.

Bonus idea ★

Place QR codes at each location that link to a geographical question to answer.

Eyes were invented before maps

"It's one of Sir's mantras!"

On the whole, young people can be hopeless at noticing what is around them, let alone being able to 'read' the by doing without clipboards and instead allowing them to get their phones out, students will be more inclined to spot what's around them and then record their ideas using the audio recorder feature.

Taking it further

There are a number of free phone apps that allow the user to record audio over images of an area. These can provide the basis for producing an annotated photo back in school.

I'm well known for uttering – well bellowing – 'Eyes were invented before maps!' and this stems from my time as an outdoor instructor. Basically, it's much easier to observe your surroundings without the distraction of a worksheet and map.

One of the most underused features of the mobile device is the audio recorder. When out on a field trip, get students to sit down and for two minutes of silence (bliss!) ask them to look around them. Next, get students to record their observations using the audio recorder on their mobile device (on an iPhone, go to settings > voice memos). You'll be amazed at what they spot, e.g.

- signs banning BBQs or warning cyclists and kiteboarders of fines
- the fact that the toilets seem to have won 'loo of the year' three years running
- where fences are located
- that the weather is awful
- the fact that there is no one around and those who are all seem to be over 65 years old or trying to entertain an infant.

These can then be revisited back in the classroom and expanded, e.g. the field trip took place during the school day – this explains the lack of teenagers and working-age adults.

School profile

"I was far more confident in the field after practising at school."

Some fieldwork techniques such as beach profiling can be complicated to teach off-site. Use lesson time to practise beach profiling and time spent on location will be more profitable.

It's clear that we get better at doing things through practice. We are also more likely to remember techniques that we have repeatedly practised, which is essential with the move away from controlled assessment towards fieldwork examinations. It means that students have to have a better understanding of fieldwork.

Gather together a set of beach profiling equipment, then find a suitable location around the school to teach the technique. Any spot with some changes in height is ideal, and the edge of a playing field or path serves as a good high tide mark. I've even seen beach profiling being practised in the school hall when it was pouring down with rain outside!

Many other fieldwork techniques can be taught and revisited on hyphen site, such as groyne measurements and number plate analysis.

Teaching tip

It's worth pre-teaching a number of students in the class before the lesson, if possible.

Bonus idea ★

Bring in a box full of shingle so that students can practise their sediment analysis.

On-site weathering

"Make use of the school's site."

The difference between erosion and weathering is commonly confused by students. Most school sites provide the opportunity to search out evidence of weathering processes in action and reinforces the point that the processes happen in situ.

Taking it further

A visit to a local church and graveyard provides an excellent location to repeat this exercise, but remind students to behave respectfully before you set out.

After you've explained the different weathering processes, get students to rummage around the school site to see if they can find any examples.

- Biological: hunt around walls that surround the fields; I've often spotted small roots and plants that have latched on to them and weakened the structure. I've even found insects and small mammals that have burrowed into the walls, breaking off chunks. Most of the schools that I have worked in have also been home to lichen which produce chemical reactions that slowly weather the stone.
- Chemical: with the reliability of rain in Britain, there is a strong likelihood that there will be evidence of some rock dissolving. This may be tricky in shiny new builds, but a good hunt around the school usually produces something of use.
- Physical: this is difficult to find as most buildings and areas won't suffer from freeze thaw action, but it's always worth a look.

By using the school grounds, that usually have an absence of moving water or ice, students are more likely to grasp the difference between erosion and weathering.

Skype in the classroom

"Speak to actual scientists who are in the field!"

Skype is a wonderful, freely available tool that brings experts into your classroom. This idea provides enrichment to lessons as well as providing inspiration for the careers that geography can take your students into in the future.

I love teaching about faraway places like the Arctic, but it's always difficult to convey what the place is actually like for the scientist or geographer working there.

The 'guest speakers' in Microsoft's 'Skype in the Classroom' (http://bit.ly/2czB564) and others like Digital Explorer (http://bit.ly/2cz1j7l) provide opportunities for teachers to connect to real-life geographers around the world. This is best used as part of a scheme of work and when students have the chance to research the person and their work to prepare unique questions only the interviewee can answer. This idea is great for opening students' minds and get them aspiring to university.

Some other ideas:

- Classroom to classroom – Create the opportunity for classes from different schools to deliver presentations to one another via Skype. Develop their literacy skills by getting them to try to include as many geographical words as possible.
- Virtual field trips – it's possible to connect to a wide range of people all over the world, and it's likely that by using 'Skype in the Classroom', you'll be able to find someone living in the location that the class are currently studying.

Teaching tip

Using Skype needs some forethought; finding the person to talk to is relatively easy, however it takes a while to plan in the lesson and link into a sequence of lessons or scheme of work to get the maximum benefit.

Bonus idea ★

Use Skype to link to your primary feeder schools. Older students can teach a topic via Skype and younger students can present their work, e.g. secondary students could teach a river flood case study to a primary class. It's far easier to organise than getting time out of the classroom.

Part 4

Creativity

The story of my life

"This helped me to remember the difference between push and pull factors for my exam."

Migration is often a hot topic and students often confuse push and pull factors, especially in exam conditions. Instead of using abstract, textbook examples, create a story about your life or that of a well-known person.

Geography is everywhere and affects everyone. When teaching migration, think about the places that you have lived and worked in. Then summarise them in a story, together with a push and pull factor or two for each one. There's no need to go into every detail, or to use real addresses, but students find a personal story a little easier to remember.

- From birth to age 14: lived in Meardy, then moved because the mine in which my father was working closed down.
- Aged 16: moved to Pencoed because my mum and dad split up.
- Aged 18–20: lived and worked in the USA because I wanted to see the world and wasn't sure what I wanted to study at university.
- Aged 28: moved to Worthing because I had family there to provide childcare...

By giving these little snippets, students can expand on the ideas themselves and ask questions for more information, e.g. being under 18 meant that there was no real choice about moving.

If you're not comfortable sharing your own life, investigate a well-known person and summarise their story. A good example is Barack Obama. Local football teams can often provide a range of ideas.

Teaching tip

Create a tour in Google Earth of your life story, putting a placemark in each location. This can then be used to describe your movements and reinforce students' use of compass directions, continents and countries.

Bonus idea ★

For homework, ask students to map the birth places of a premiership football team or a film cast, together with where they live now.

Beat the teacher!

"One of these days I'm going to get to the answer!"

Teachers are often quick to give the right answer to the students without giving them the opportunity to figure it out themselves. By allowing the class to work as a team in order to ask you questions and guess the answer, you'll not only be developing their enquiry skills but also ensuring that they listen to each other.

Teaching tip

This idea works best if you save the learning objectives and lesson title until after the story is revealed.

Start a lesson with a mystery image, headline or video to introduce the topic and provide a hook. Showing an image of a ghost town in Death Valley or a fishing boat on top of a house in New Orleans, for instance, can spark interest and get students questioning and hypothesising. The class will buzz as they try to figure out the story behind the image.

Allow the class to ask you ten questions. They don't have to be answered 'yes' or 'no', indeed it is better if they aren't. The questions should be linked to the image. Expect the whole class to listen to your answers carefully and ensure their next question builds upon the previous answer. Give out rewards for great questions.

Be patient and persevere. It's a good tip to allow the class to 'think, pair, write, share' (see Idea 93) after each question and encourage them not to guess. After the ten questions, ask the students to write a short paragraph outlining the story behind the image. To make the students think even harder, consider banning certain questions such as, 'Where is it?' and 'What happened?'.

Taking it further

Involve the whole class by randomly choosing a student to ask the question. This keeps everyone listening and thinking!

Does Iceland exist?

"Although I thought that this idea was nuts to start with, it really does develop their research and reasoning skills."

Today, masses and masses of information is readily available over the internet. The trouble we have as teachers is that students don't always give much thought to how reliable that information is. This activity challenges a class to really think about what they find online.

I came across some early work by guerrilla geographer Daniel Raven-Ellison, where he'd asked students to prove that New Zealand existed. From this, and a newspaper article about islands made up by Dutch explorers, spawned the lesson sequence: does Iceland exist?

At the end of a unit on Iceland, open the lesson with an image of a location in Iceland and the question: 'Is it possible to prove a place exists when you've never been there?' After a couple of minutes' discussion, 'Does Iceland exist?' is written on the board. This could go for any country or place being studied in geography and is great for deepening knowledge around case study locations.

The next stage is to get the students to each make a 30 second micro-presentation that proves that Iceland exists. You'll be surprised at the inventiveness of the class, e.g. some will visit the webcams in the country before comparing their images to the weather forecast; others will find information about Iceland and how the 2010 volcanic eruption affected most of Europe. The point is that they have to find multiple, high-quality sources of information.

Teaching tip

This idea works best if there is access to computers or mobile devices. However, if they aren't available simply collect resources such as travel guides, atlases, newspaper articles and textbooks about the place for students to cross-reference. Even better, take them to the school library and set them loose.

Curiosity glasses

"You'll never look at sticky notes in the same way again."

One of the most difficult skills to develop in geography is empathy for different groups of people, and writing balanced accounts from differing points of view. By having a little fun and removing the risk of saying something wrong, it's possible to get your students to think differently.

Teenagers are notoriously worried about their image, and many find it difficult to write about different points of view. Grab a set of sticky notes and create some curiosity glasses.

- Fold two notes in half so the sticky tab is on both halves.
- Carefully tear out two squares from the centre of each note.
- Unfold each note and stick them to your face, just above your eyebrows.
- You're now wearing curiosity glasses!

Yes, I'm afraid you're going to have to look silly for a while for this one! When wearing curiosity glasses, it's possible to transform into an alter ego. Use the glasses:

- When self- or peer-assessing work or decoding a GCSE exam question, where students become the examiner.
- During group work: each student can take on a different persona to consider different points of view around a particular topic.
- During fieldwork: students can become the environment agency or the local landowner.

This idea works because it removes the peer pressure that comes with role play, it's fun and it marks the point at which they need to consider other points of view.

Taking it further

In a six-mark question where students have to give at least two different points of view, set a timer. The class wear a set of curiosity glasses for the first three minutes and then remove them for the second three minutes, using the glasses to remind them to consider different points of view and to check their answer carefully.

Curriculum hackers!

"Being allowed to change lessons really developed my passion for geography and showed me that geographers can change the world!"

'Student voice' is a term often bandied about, but often it doesn't go much beyond tokenistic surveys. By getting students involved in the curriculum-making process, they take ownership over lessons and help develop sequences of learning that meet their needs more closely.

The scheme of work is a very important document, although it's easy to miss the needs of some students or deliver units that hold little interest to the local geographies of the school community. Start this activity by surveying your students: ask which topics they enjoyed, which they found difficult and how confident they were at tackling the assessments. The beauty of this is that you never know what it will uncover!

The next stage is the most important: use that information to ask students to help develop the curriculum. This is quite straightforward and can be completed in three to four sessions.

- The first lesson should focus on the needs and wants of the students. Whilst most want loads of trips, they know that it isn't realistic or feasible.
- Next, show the students your schemes of work and explain the terminology.
- The following sessions should be really focussed, e.g. getting exam skills into a topic on urban development or embedding homework effectively.
- Allow students to make small changes to existing documents.

Trust your students and you'll be surprised and delighted by what they come up with! And remember, there is often far more flexibility in the curriculum than you think!

Teaching tip

Remember that teachers are professionals and you should use your judgement. For example, explain that the specification and curriculum must be met.

Peer teaching

"In-school research has shown that students who teach others remember more when it comes to exam time."

Peer teaching is a powerful tool when used well as part of the sequences of a lesson, and is particularly effective when disadvantaged students are asked to take the stage.

Teaching tip

Keep accurate records of the impact of the peer teaching in order to evaluate effectively and to convince colleagues to join in.

Many teachers shy away from peer teaching as it can to be difficult to set up and control. But by establishing a clear structure this idea can be very effective and has been proven to work both within the same class and between classes.

Peer teaching works best in small groups or pairs. Set a clearly defined area to teach – case studies often work well, since there are clear facts to remember and a clear scaffold available as most follow the 'causes, effects, responses' pattern.

Next, provide some resources and ask students to prepare a lesson for their peers. I find this works best when using material that is not familiar. They should aim to plan a 15–20 minute session. Don't be overgenerous with the preparation time or the students can lose focus. Around 10–15 minutes of prep time works well. The students can create a number of resources but they don't have to be fancy – a simple worksheet is often as effective as a complex animation.

Finally, allow the students to teach each other, sharing their newly found knowledge about the subject. Ensure that learning is consolidated by using a suitable assessment question either for homework or at the end of the lesson. When you revisit questions on the same topic in the future, you'll find that the student teachers will have retained more information.

Taking it further

Ask students to teach primary school children as part of transition arrangements.

Primary marking

"When the older students knew that younger children would be marking their work, they worked harder to ensure that they produced something to be proud of."

Secondary geographers can learn a great deal from primary colleagues, and their classes present an ideal opportunity to build links between schools and start the transition journey.

For this idea, you'll need a willing primary class who are doing a similar topic. In this example, the primary class were exploring the geomorphology of rivers.

The first stage was to provide the primary age children with work created by the older students. This inspired the younger children, and raised their expectations. The children marked the older students' work for spelling, punctuation and grammar (SPaG) as well as looking at how clearly the ideas were explained. The secondary students benefitted from this as they paid particular attention to the presentation of their work as well as endeavouring to use the appropriate geographical terms.

Next, the older students marked the younger children's work, looking for quality geography to comment on. Both sets of students need to be provided with clear success criteria to mark against so that their comments are informed and appropriate. This use of structure and scaffolding, and subsequent conversations between the students, is where the key learning took place.

Teaching tip

Get the students to write their comments on sticky notes using the simple 'What went well'/'even better if' format. That way, comments can be checked and quickly changed if needed.

Textbook transformation

"This idea saved me hours of planning and reinventing the wheel."

Textbooks are every geography teacher's guilty pleasure as they contain a wealth of information and resources. This idea uses textbook information to challenge students to create something new, remembering the key facts in the process.

Teaching tip

This is a great activity for revision sessions and I'd recommend making copies of the best ones, scanning them in and then making them available on the school's intranet or library.

Many students revise simply by reading through old material and highlighting parts of it, so it is very important that we model new revision techniques, such as this one, which uses textbooks in a novel way.

Textbooks have one major drawback: the case studies quickly become out of date. However, this idea can be used effectively for any current geographical event for which you have a textbook page for a similar event from the past, e.g.

- local planning issues
- river and coastal flooding events
- earthquakes, volcanoes and other natural disasters
- localising retail and urban morphology case studies for your local area.

Take the textbook case study, e.g. a two-page spread on Hurricane Katrina. Create a blank A3 template that copies the layout of the textbook; most books will have a great mixture of text, images and graphs that are easy for students to follow. Students fill in the template with information about their own up to date case study, e.g. on the latest hurricane to hit the USA.

Taking it further

Encourage students to check the publication date of the textbook as this helps them become media savvy as well as being able to assess the reliability of the book.

At the end of the activity, the students have a well-structured case study example that is up to date.

Meet and greet

"Setting a clear routine at the start of lessons puts learning first."

Often, one of the biggest barriers to learning is creating a climate that is conducive to study. The signals that you give out within the first five minutes can make or break a lesson. Develop a strong routine and stick to it consistently and students will soon acclimatise.

Following a similar pattern at the beginning of every lesson has the effect of ensuring that the class gets on task quickly and that no learning time is lost.

- Stand at the door and greet each student as they come in. Aim to say something to each person. This welcomes them to your space and also allows an opportunity to defuse any situations at the door. Keep a careful eye on their uniform and equipment, as picking up on these things sends the signal that you focus on the small details.
- Have an activity ready to go. Either hand this out to each student as you greet them, or have it clearly displayed. The activity should be simple and require no instruction to start. My routine is to get the class to write the date and title and then do the activity, which should link the learning of the previous lesson to this one.
- Appoint students to carry out simple tasks such as giving out books.
- Close the door. This marks the point at which any stragglers are late. Walk around the room checking that students are on task and pick up or help anyone who isn't. Avoid the temptation to get into conversation here.
- Take the register before moving onto the next phase of the lesson.

I find that using this routine settles the class quickly. Taking time to develop this social capital with each class will pay dividends.

Teaching tip

Don't be tempted to deviate from the routine, staying consistent makes it much easier to keep expectations high and identify misdemeanours.

Floating topicality

"I don't know why I was so afraid of deviating from the scheme of work."

Research has demonstrated that revisiting topics helps students to remember the key facts more consistently. This is the perfect justification to pause the curriculum in order to explore any current news events that will deepen geographical knowledge.

Teaching tip

If you are part of a larger department, work out a rota for developing resources around particular topics. Once there are a number of templates in place, it's a relatively simple activity to update them with the key information.

Any official curriculum is only ever part of the overall school curriculum, and sometimes it isn't always as creative or inspiring as it could be. You, however, can be both these things! One of the unique features of geography is that the subject is happening all around us all of the time and therefore current events will mirror the topics and units that we explore. 'Floating topicality' is a term coined by former Hampshire Geography Adviser, Jeff Stanfield, and relates to the idea of pausing the curriculum in order to explore current events.

When a major event has happened, such as the devastating floods in north-east England in 2015, it's relatively easy to get some simple resources together. The Geographical Association and Royal Geographical Society, for example, both swiftly produce ideas around current events. Revisiting topics when they occur in real time allows students to reacquaint themselves with the main geographical processes and knowledge whilst giving them a real-world context. Pausing the curriculum is even useful for exam classes, as they are able to practise recalling key information and applying their knowledge.

Taking it further

Floating topicality can also be semi-planned. For example, the period around April to May usually sees at least one major news story about Everest, whilst exploring the effects of tourism is covered better during the summer.

Floating topicality ensures that we meet our responsibility as geographers to help young people decode and engage with the world around them whilst developing sound examination skills.

Rubbish map

"We made a real difference to our school!"

Litter is often a big issue in schools. Turn your students into campaigners by creating some action art!

This is a simple idea to illustrate how much litter is thrown away. There are two options, depending on how much of an issue litter is in your school: the first is to collect litter from around the school; the second, if your school grounds are always immaculate, is to collect litter from non-recycling bins. You'll have to get the students to tool up with gloves and litter pickers, and keep it to the dry stuff such as food packaging and bottles.

Once you have a stash of rubbish, find a space where you can make a collage of the world. The scale and location of your map will depend on how brave you are and how much litter you get, e.g. it's quite possible to get enough material for a classroom-sized map over a day!

The next stage is to create the map collage from the rubbish and display it somewhere prominent. In the past I've used them in assemblies, or put them on display in the corridor. After the map is in place, it's time to start campaigning. Get students to use the map as a resource to convince others to reduce their waste.

Taking it further

This is an ideal activity that can be adapted into the focus for a geography club.

Little notices

"This was a fun activity and felt naughty although I learned a lot about my school."

How much do your students really notice about their school environment? This idea gets them to take a much closer look at their built environment and even challenges them to do something about it.

Teaching tip

The follow up is important and should be well structured, using suitable writing frames if relevant.

Places affect people: their moods and actions are often dictated by the spaces that they work and live in. Get the class to close their eyes and listen silently. What do they notice about the classroom that they hadn't before, e.g. inside sounds – the projector fan, the footsteps of people above them; outside sounds – birdsong, traffic, aeroplanes high above them.

Explain that the purpose of 'little notices' is to spot features around the school that usually go unseen and which could be improved, and stick a little notice up to draw attention to it.

There are three phases for this activity that may span a sequence of lessons.

• Agree the rules
Little notices is an example of guerrilla geography, where geographers try to change an area for the better. Although it may feel a little cheeky, it must always be safe and never offensive. The activity flirts around the rules rather than breaks them and, most importantly, the outcome must generate thought.

• Reconnaissance
Get the students to walk around the school and look for things that they haven't spotted before. It's best if you assign different parts of the school to different groups. They need to study the area in detail, reading notices and

looking for other features. It's important that pupils understand why they feel strongly about what they see, e.g. one class spotted that:

- most of the notices in their school were commands that suggested that students couldn't be trusted
- signage in the school was mostly in the English language despite the fact that the school's community spanned over 30 different languages
- there was only one plant inside the building.

• Action

Students should make official-looking notices that point out what they have seen. Check the notices first and then allow them to be stuck up around school, e.g.

- 'Is there room for individuality?'
- 'Why is this plant being held prisoner?'
- 'Why is nobody looking?' (Placed in a spot where bullying occurred.)

One group started to cover up the English language signs with those in different languages.

Follow up the activity with a blog post or article in the student newspaper explaining the action. Get the headteacher to listen to the arguments presented by your class and make changes to the school.

Bonus idea ★

Getting students out doing doorstep geography within lesson time is important but can lead to confusion when most schools don't want students out. Sending an email can often clog already full inboxes, so issue each individual with a lanyard and badge saying that they are out of lesson on important geography fieldwork. On the reverse of the badge, put a list of expectations when carrying out fieldwork.

Navigating the school as...

"I never appreciated the effect that the built environment has on different groups."

Getting across the needs of different groups of people to teenagers is challenging as their world view is dictated by their own experiences. This doorstep geography idea allows students to evaluate their school's built environment and can lead to campaigning for change.

Teaching tip

The variations in role are almost endless and a quick email to other members of staff, or a notice in the staffroom will usually bring props that can be used to make the activity more authentic.

Schools are often poorly designed for anyone that isn't part of its community, but we quickly forget their quirks when we grow accustomed to a place. Divide the class into small groups of three at most. Assign each student in the group a role:

- timer
- navigator
- note-taker.

Take the class to your main reception area and explain that the aim of the exercise is to get back to the classroom. However, they will be given certain limitations, such as:

- acting as though they don't speak English and therefore can only follow signs that have pictures
- pretending to be a teacher who is new to the school who is relying on verbal directions
- imagining they are a student in a wheelchair who can only use ramps and lifts
- have one group going round as themselves.

As the students move around the site, they should time how long it takes to get back to the classroom and map the route they took. The note-taker should write down any particular challenges that the group encountered.

The class will get a much better understanding of how the built environment can limit accessibility.

Taking it further

Invite members of the community in to the school to speak to the class about accessibility issues. Most areas have active campaigning groups. This could lead to a campaign to change the school environment in some way, such as improving signage.

Exams

Part 5

Decode the question

"Taking time to understand the question helped me know what the examiner wanted."

Geographers are required to provide clear, concise and well-supported answers to questions that can be very specific. Students, under exam conditions, often fail to answer the specific question. The solution is to teach them how to decode a question.

Teaching tip

The examiner's report is full of useful information about exam tips and performance and it is well worth familiarising yourself with it at the start of the school year.

There are a number of ways to help students to unpick questions, but one of the best is asking them to 'B.U.G.' the question:

- **B**ox the command words
- **U**nderline the geography
- **G**lance at the marks available and link to the question throughout the response.

Box the command words

It's always worth checking with your examination board about the exact terminology that you should use, however as a general rule follow this two stage process:

1. Check the key command words:

- describe – say what something is like.
- explain – give a reason for identifying the word, usually by using the connectives 'because' or 'this means that' or 'so'.
- suggest – requires the student to make links to other units or bring in their own knowledge.

2. Check for instructions from the examiner. These are usually in bold and often ignored by students who lose many marks in their rush to start writing. In case study and decision-making questions, the examiner often gives an essay structure for students to follow, e.g.

- include figures in your answer
- use map evidence

Taking it further

Become an examiner for your exam board. The training and knowledge is worth around a grade to each student as you improve your own knowledge of how to best answer the questions.

- examine figure 3 in the resource booklet
- give two points of view.

Underline the geography

This is a vital step.

- Does the question refer to social, environmental, economic or political factors?
- If the word 'people' is used, check exactly who is being referred to and always write the name of groups of people, e.g. local residents, environmentalists etc.

Glance at the marks available and link to the questions throughout the response.

- A question asking you to describe something for three marks – this often requires three simple points.
- A three-mark question that requires data to be used from a resource will always reserve at least one mark for using the data.
- A question asking you to explain something for four marks – this wants two expanded points.
- A six-mark question – this requires a balanced answer considering both the positive and negative aspects of the topic. The student will need to write at least two well-developed points.

In at the deep end

"Making examination questions part of every lesson from Year 7 onwards, raises expectations, and results in better attainment."

The traditional view is that classes should be taught the relevant geographical content before tackling an exam question. However, flipping this process around can boost students' confidence when writing in an exam-style format.

Taking it further

This idea is ideal for flipped learning. Set a homework based on the content required for an exam question. Case studies work really well for this if you issue a mind map or article. The students study the information at home and then tackle the exam question at the beginning of the following lesson. Great for revision time too!

Challenge your classes by giving them an exam question at the start of a unit, rather than at the end. The work can then be revisited once the content has been covered, and the improvement made raises the confidence of the class as they see how well they have done.

Try the following sequence in a lesson.

- Give the exam question to the class and ask them to decode the question using Idea 49.
- Next, get them to think, pair, write, share in small groups around the question (see Idea 93). In particular, encourage them to make links to their existing knowledge, any information the examiner has given (such as graphs or photographs) and previous units.
- As they write the question, build their confidence by reassuring them that this is practice.
- Finally, issue the mark scheme, getting the class to self- or peer-assess the work.

You'll find that most of the class will have picked up some marks. This is a huge boost for students when they haven't covered the content. You will also notice that their confidence in tackling exam questions grows over time. So, don't be afraid: introduce examination questions early on and remember that we need to teach exam techniques as well as the geography.

Show them your working!

"Watching the teacher construct an exam answer word by word was really useful and showed me exactly what I had to do."

Modelling is one of the most powerful tools in our teaching toolbox, especially as geography is full of extended writing, diagrams, and skills such as annotation. Showing students how to do this using a visualiser is one of the most useful activities you can do to boost progress.

Visualisers are available online for around £50 and provide a clear image on screen via a projector. They will allow you to do all of the following.

- Demonstrate how to decode a question (Idea 49) or write down your thoughts about a particular question or task. Sharing your own thoughts is very useful for students who are developing their own ways of approaching activities.
- Construct a model answer or extended piece of writing with the class, sharing your thoughts, mistakes and ideas.
- Draw a diagram stage by stage, adding details and labels as you go.
- Annotate maps, photographs and graphs with students so they can see how to interrogate a wide range of images.
- Demonstrate drawing graphs – graphs are often an area of weakness, but demonstrating how to construct them will improve this key geographical skill.
- Share OS maps and other resources so that students can see them – this idea is great for sharing textbook images too.
- Choose and show great work from your class.

By using the visualiser instead of presenting students with an already completed example or using the board, you'll be setting high expectations and modelling exactly what is needed for high quality geography.

Teaching tip

Don't be afraid to make mistakes in front of the class. They are part of learning how to cope with activities. Ask the class to look out for mistakes, for example in spelling grammar and punctuation, and model a solution, such as using a dictionary.

READ the resource

"This idea is simple and can be adapted to almost any resource."

Geography is a wonderful subject full of diverse and dynamic resources. The problem can be helping students to interrogate them in order to draw conclusions. This simple method can be adapted to almost any resource.

Teaching tip

You won't always need to include all of the steps, and they don't always need to be taken in the same order, e.g. sometimes it's worth starting with Recognise, then Describe before Explain and Analyse.

For any resource, teach students the following pattern.

Recognise

- What type of resource are you looking at? (E.g. satellite image, photograph, news story, etc.)
- What does the resource show?
- What information is provided by the resource?
- Write some basic points about what you are looking at.

Explain

- Is there any information that explains what you have already spotted?
- Does the information presented help answer the main enquiry question?

Analyse

- What are the positives and negatives presented by the resource?
- Are there different points of view provided?
- Who created the resource? Is it reliable?

Describe

- What does the resource show?
- What physical and human geography is visible?

Taking it further

Consider creating a display that lists the multitude of geographical resources in use in lessons together with an example of each.

By using this approach each time, you'll find that students will quickly be able to access and interrogate any resource presented to them as well as assess the usefulness of the information it provides.

PEEL

"This approach really improved the persuasive writing of my class and has resulted in more complex answers."

Many students are often very good at writing a few simple points but then stop short of expanding on their answers. PEEL gives a simple structure to writers so that the quality of their writing improves, gaining more depth and therefore greater quality.

PEEL stands for Point, Evidence, Explain, Link. Using PEEL tackles two areas which students have trouble developing in high-quality geographical writing: they often forget to include evidence or fail to explain their answers as detailed explanations.

- **Point** – make a simple point, which may often come from a resource such as a map, e.g. 'Earthquakes are concentrated along the boundaries of tectonic plates'.
- **Evidence** – add evidence by quoting information from sources, e.g. 'such as along the Mid-Atlantic Ridge around Iceland where the Eurasian and North American plates meet.' This stage is great for case studies as it encourages the students to include place-specific information.
- **Explain** – explain by adding theory to the answer, e.g. 'This is because friction builds up along the divergent plate boundary, building up pressure. When this pressure is released by a sudden plate movement, the resulting energy creates an earthquake close to the boundary.'
- **Link** – finally, link the point to the question or to another unit using a connective, e.g. 'Therefore, earthquakes are more likely to occur close to plate boundaries where pressure builds up whereas further away from plate boundaries it is less likely for earthquakes to occur.'

Teaching tip

PEEL is most effective when it is being used across a whole department right the way from Year 7. That way, students will develop engrained habits that they will take with them into the examination.

Which means that

"All I had in my mind when tackling those longer questions was Sir saying, 'Which means that......'!"

This is another simple idea that encourages students to expand on their answers, resulting in better quality geographical writing and higher marks.

Teaching tip

It's best to model this approach by expanding one of the simple points first with the class using a visualiser. Don't worry too much if the connectives seem awkward at first, over time students will learn to create flowing sentences and be able to link the ideas together.

This example uses the hydrological cycle, but it is easily adapted to other topics that require students to expand upon simple statements, e.g. retail locations, flood defences and migration. First, ensure the knowledge is covered. In this case, students examined a number of photographs for factors that would increase flooding. The class came up with:

- steep slopes
- deforested area used for sheep farming
- impermeable rock
- many tributaries
- saturated soil.

By placing the factors in a table and asking students to expand upon each one, referring to the hydrological cycle and using the simple connective 'which means that', their answers were significantly improved. For example:

'The area is deforested and used for sheep farming, which means that there are fewer interceptions making precipitation reach the ground quicker so that there is not time for it to infiltrate into the soil. This means that there is a greater chance of flooding.'

This is particularly effective for lower attainers as it enables them to write better answers using a clear scaffold upon which to expand simple points.

Simplify the case studies

"I found that I was able to answer the case study questions easily as I had all of the facts I needed."

Case study questions are a common feature of geography exams and are amongst the most challenging questions for students to answer as they require them to memorise lots of facts that are easily mixed up and confused. By simplifying case studies to a few pertinent and useful facts, you'll find that students will tackle them with more confidence.

I found teaching case studies tricky until I attended a TeachMeet and listened to Ben Crocket, the lead geography teacher at Durrington High School, explain his approach. Since adapting and using the idea, I can firmly recommend it.

Students are far more likely to commit information to their long-term memory if it is simplified and transformed into a diagram. This will then free up their working memory to tackle the exam question by making links and expanding the points in relevant ways.

Model to your class how to construct a case study diagram.

- Take the time to work out what information is required and ensure that the exam board's specific terminology is used.
- Keep the pictures simple, and use symbols and single words rather than sentences.
- Give the case study a title and note the relevant command words.
- Try to create links wherever possible to help students to remember place-specific information.
- Place specific information on relevant parts of the diagram and add titles, e.g. causes and effects.

Teaching tip

Don't be tempted to show a completed version of the diagram on a PowerPoint slide, as modelling its construction and the conversations and opportunities for questioning are far more effective when drawn with the students.

Taking it further

Keep the diagrams as simple as possible and don't be tempted to get students to design their own as this leads to misconceptions. Revisit the diagrams often and you'll soon find that your classes will be answering case study questions with relative ease.

Bing OS maps

"Freely available Ordnance Survey mapping of the whole UK? What's not to like?!"

The maps on bing.com provide 1:25,000 and 1:50,000 Ordnance Survey mapping of the UK for free.

Teaching tip

Ask students to use bing.com maps in order to explore the services in an urban area.

Simply visit bing.com and select 'Maps'. Navigate to the location that you wish to explore and then select 'Ordnance Survey' from the drop down list of maps at the top right of the screen. Then simply zoom in to the area to reveal the two different map layers.

You can use this approach in the following ways:

- Ask students to compare the information contained on the different map layers, e.g. compare the OS map layer with the road layer. Which information is missing? What audience is each layer primarily for? What are the advantages and disadvantages of each?
- Compare the area around your school with a contrasting location, e.g. compare rural with urban or suburban with inner city.
- Start the lesson with the OS map layer showing and then ask students to predict what the area will look like when the satellite layer is selected. What information is missing? Which is the best resource for identifying land use?
- Visit fieldwork sites virtually, and ask students to write a description of the area from the OS map layer.

By using the OS map layer in Bing, it's possible to explore various locations all around the United Kingdom, and with the increased focus on the country in the curriculum, this will add interest to your lessons.

Memorise that!

"Although repetitive, I found that I remembered information more easily."

Research shows that students are far more likely to remember information if they revisit it often. This simple approach supports students in committing information to their long-term memory.

This idea works for diagrams, such as an explanation of longshore drift, or for other information and facts. There are at least three stages.

Stage one involves you teaching the material by modelling it to the students, and them copying and annotating it with you. This is great when combined with a visualiser.

The second stage is to expose the students to a quick recall of the information, ideally 30–40 minutes after coming across the ideas for the first time. Get them to draw or write from memory and, if needed, set homework to fill in any gaps.

The next stage should occur about one–two weeks after first learning the material. Ask the class to draw or write from memory and then quickly assess who has remembered the most and who needs more support. Go over the information again, ensuring that any knowledge gaps are filled, and test the class again at the end of the lesson.

This process can be used time and again and will help students to remember key facts, information and diagrams.

Taking it further

Although not exciting, holding regular spelling and key term definition tests are a great way of helping students to commit geographical terms to their long-term memory, especially as many longer questions carry marks for accurate spelling, punctuation and grammar. Keep revisiting material covered over the entire course as opposed to limiting questions to the recently studied units.

Give a lesson a different language

"I now appreciate how difficult it is migrating to a different country."

Lessons are mainly delivered through the English language but modern technology and apps allow us to change this, letting our students experience life for those whose first language is not English.

Teaching tip

Although this idea works best with access to the internet via mobile or desktop devices, a stash of language dictionaries can also be used for a non-tech version.

I'll always remember walking into a colleague's geography lesson at Priory School to be greeted by the following:

Dowiadujemy się o kilku różnych językach, które są wypowiedziane w Priory School.

Będziesz w stanie:
1. Pracy w zespole
2. Przeczytaj mapy
3. Użyj technologii mobilnych w celu zbadania.

There were looks of bewilderment amongst the class, although if you have a mobile device you should be able to figure out the meaning quickly enough. Tools such as Google Translate and easy access to the internet mean that we can now bring language in to the classroom with far more ease than was previously possible. Prepare your first slide and starter instructions in a different language or set up a trail of clues all in different languages.

Taking it further

Ask the students to write about how they felt. Can they adapt this experience to be able to empathise with refugees arriving in a new country?

This helps students to empathise with those from different parts of the world as well as developing their problem-solving skills. The idea can also include any students whose first language is not English, empowering them to become more involved in the lesson.

Interrogating the ads

"I now question everything. Even the teacher!"

Sometimes students are guilty of making the wildest of generalisations based upon the flimsiest of evidence. Use the adverts on the internet to illustrate the importance of questioning the data.

Get on YouTube and search for some adverts. The best to use are from well-known cosmetic companies and haircare products. Be sure to get some examples that represent both genders. Next, play the clips to the class. You'll get some strange looks, but ask them to identify the main claims from the advert, e.g. 'users prefer our product over everything else' or 'strengthens your hair and covers grey.' I'm sure that you know the type of thing.

Next, play the advert again only this time pause the clip when the small print shows up. These adverts are great because most of the claims are based upon very small sample numbers, e.g. '78% of 52 users agreed.' This is a brilliant and accessible illustration of how data can be manipulated to strengthen an argument. Ask the class if such a sample size is representative of the 70 million people living in the UK. Is it reliable? Who conducted the research and is it quoted?

The conversation can then move on to how one identifies whether a source is reliable and helps students interrogate even the most scientific-looking of sources.

Taking it further

Encourage students to always 'tag' their claims with the source of information and the sample size. Doing so from the first lesson in Year 7 will ensure that they develop the habit of quoting sources of information.

Silent disco

"A great idea for exploring distinctive landscapes."

Geographers often have to compare and contrast different locations in terms of their physical and human features. Go one step further by engaging your class in the emotion of the place . . . and make the classroom silent at the same time!

Teaching tip

Check your school's policy on the use of mobile devices before running this activity. Check that any music tracks you listen to or research lyrics for are suitable.

It's important to allow students to engage with the emotion of a place. Choose two or more contrasting locations, or alternatively contrasting photographs of the same location (e.g. a before and after photo of the site of an earthquake). This idea also works well when exploring urban morphology showing a selection of images from the same city.

Ask students to get out their mobile devices and open up their music app and select a track that matches each photograph. Make sure they listen to the entire track to be sure that it is appropriate and matches the location.

Scaffold the next stage of the activity with the following questions:

- What can you see?
- How would you feel?
- What would you smell?
- What would you be able to hear?
- Would there be any tastes?

Taking it further

This idea is also great when out in the field. When you first arrive at a location, give the students a few minutes to sit down and select a track. Follow this up with a section in their field notebook to write about their choice.

Students should discuss these questions, justifying or revising their choice of track for the location. Finally, ask the students to write about their choice, linking their track selection to the location's geographical features – sometimes looking up the lyrics can help with this.

You'll find that your classes will be able to empathise and improve their imagination of unfamiliar places, and gain lots of practice in identifying human and physical features.

Geographical rucksack

"I never realised just how many different points of view existed in each class."

Everyone's view of the world is slightly different because of their personal experiences, viewpoints and beliefs. The geographical rucksack allows student's own thoughts and viewpoints be shared in a safe environment.

One of the most important aspects of geography is to take into account the many different viewpoints from around the world, and this should start in your own classroom. You'll find that within every class there will exist several different points of view about the same place. This idea works equally well at any scale, e.g.

- your classroom
- your school, or a particular location
- your local area or city
- an unknown location, such as a far-flung case study location.

Allow the class to explore some resources about the chosen area then give out sticky notes and ask each student to write down at least five things about that place. It's best to keep them to single words or short phrases and to place each point on a separate note.

Collect the notes in and use a word cloud generator like wordle.net to create a great visual representation of the information. Follow this up next lesson by asking students to select words and phrases that they were surprised by, which they related to the most, and if they disagreed with any.

Over time, you'll open up students' misconceptions and minds as the anonymous word cloud creates a safe environment within which to explore new ideas.

Taking it further

With older students who you know well, it's possible to interrogate their thoughts and discuss the possible reasons for differences in opinion or perspective.

Take 5

"This is a great way to gauge perceptions of an area."

Within your class there will be many different points of view. This idea will demonstrate this in a simple way, and creates a fantastic learning display in the process.

Teaching tip

This is often the first activity that I get students to do after first arriving at a fieldwork location (well, after they've all been to the loo and staff have had a coffee...). This captures their first impressions of a place and develops their ability to 'read' the landscape.

Taking it further

When on a residential trip or fieldtrip, give a digital camera to one chosen student to capture their point of view of the trip. The images are often great for selling overseas trips as well as seeing a different perspective of your time away.

Bonus idea ★

When away on fieldwork or a residential trip, set a student photo competition. You'll soon have loads of high-quality images.

Images are everywhere and most secondary school-aged students walk around with a portable device capable of capturing their views of the world. In order to get students to appreciate different viewpoints, ask each student to take five images around a shared focus, e.g.

- local shopping areas
- the school grounds
- the classroom
- a fieldwork location.

The beauty of this activity is that it can be used in lessons, in fieldwork or set as homework. Explain to the class that they should think carefully about the images they take and not just snap away, as they're only allowed five to represent the area. They will need to use their geographical skills to think about what to take.

Next, get the students to share their images by emailing them to you or printing them out. Collages can then be created. This activity is also great for developing better-annotated images of a particular location – these can be produced in the classroom.

Finally, consider having an exhibition or producing a slideshow that brings home the idea that different people often have different perspectives on the same thing.

Command word bingo

"Students' exam answers improved markedly after repeating this activity regularly."

One of the biggest barriers for students when decoding exam questions is understanding the command words. Ensure that your classes are familiar with them by using this bingo idea regularly across the curriculum.

The meaning of command words needs to be explicitly taught to students and they should have the opportunity to practise them often. Head over to your exam board's website and you will find a glossary of command words. Understanding these is key to success across the entire curriculum. Once in receipt of this information, it's time for some bingo.

First create some bingo grids. I find that 3 x 3 grids work best in terms of the balance between time and learning. Ask the class to select nine command words from a list that is provided on the board. They should end up with something like this:

Explain	Outline	Describe
Suggest	Analyse	State

Next, read the definition of each command word out in a random order, e.g.

- to give a reason for
- to give the advantages and disadvantages of the situation.

If an individual has that word, they cross it out. The winner is the first to get all nine words crossed out. This idea can also be reversed so that students have a grid of definitions and you read out the command word.

Teaching tip

This is an idea that works best when repeated regularly as a low-stake, high-frequency test. Throw them in at the beginning and end of lessons and always have a stack of grids available, or simply get students to write nine words down in the back of their exercise book.

Taking it further

Don't limit command word bingo to examination classes, but also ensure that assessments lower down the school mirror the command words used in the high-stakes exams. That way, responding in the appropriate way will become second nature to the students.

Feedback

Part 6

IDEA 64

Questions as feedback

"Simple differentiation and student response in one."

Research shows that effective feedback really makes a difference in improving outcomes, however, geographers often teach many classes and marking can be time consuming. This idea saves time and ensures that every student knows what they need to do to improve.

Teaching tip

Don't see this idea as triple marking which sucks up time. During the beginning of the lesson, wander around with a pen and assess the students' responses. This allows you to help students even more. It's also worth providing the original resources for the class.

Checking work is a crucially important activity to do. However, it's not necessary to write detailed comments in every book, as this can take forever. Firstly, target the piece of work and the particular aspect of geography you want to have a close look at, e.g. developing students understanding of life in shanty settlements.

Whilst you read through the work, instead of leaving detailed comments on each piece, leave questions based upon the level of work. The questions can be tailored to the individual, providing differentiation, support and challenge, e.g.

- Can you describe two additional features of living in a shanty settlement?
- How is the quality of life of residents affected in this settlement? Link to development indicators.

At the start of the next lesson, give the class five minutes to answer your questions. This closes the gap between where the students were and where they could be.

Different starters

"This idea ensured that I provided the right level of challenge or support for every student."

When looking over students' work, it's often clear that some individuals have ended the previous lesson with a different level of understanding to others. Some will be ready to move on, whilst others still need to grapple with the basics. This idea allows the teacher to provide the right level of support for every student.

Geography classes are often mixed ability with wildly different levels of numeracy, literacy and prior attainment. This can make starting the next lesson in the sequence difficult: how do we ensure that the needs of every student are supported? I realised that one way was to set different activities for students as they walk through the door (see Idea 44).

Read the class's work from the week before, and decide how each student will start the next lesson. Develop a range of activities for the students to start straight away. Don't give them a choice, otherwise those who require more challenge often elect to do an activity within their comfort zone. I communicate the tasks using a symbol (e.g. square, triangle etc.) instead of 'gold, silver, bronze', so that individuals don't really know the purpose behind the groupings, e.g.

- For those who had trouble communicating the basics – a sheet of key words for the students to define each geographical term.
- For those who understood the work – a graph or alternative resource to give an opportunity to apply their knowledge to a new situation.
- For those who need a more challenging activity – an activity to link their work to another aspect of geography and their own knowledge.
- For those that have written a one-sided account – a task to write from the other point of view.

Taking it further

Use your marking to mix up the seating plan now and again, e.g. you could sit all of those who are struggling together for a few lessons so that you can give them the extra support whilst those that are ready to move on tackle a more challenging activity.

Mark PP first

"By checking the books of those students not making progress, I was able to tackle the issues and provide them with effective feedback."

Research suggests that feedback is most effective when it is given just at the right time, when the student can make the correction quickly. The problem with waiting to mark a whole set of books is that often those that will benefit most from your feedback have to wait too long. This simple tweak to your routine will allow you to pick up on errors and correct them swiftly.

Taking it further

When marking, make a note of the concepts and ideas that students have struggled with, then use this to inform your planning of the next lesson. Using symbols to identify which concept each student needs to practice will help you to effectively differentiate your next lesson according to each student's needs.

From experience and conducting action research in the school I've worked in, students from disadvantaged backgrounds are less likely to be asked at home about their learning and less likely to have someone at home that can help them or praise them. It struck me that if I stuck to my marking timetable, some students would miss out on getting the feedback when they most needed it.

Check these students' books after each lesson or, even better, at some point within the lesson. This allows you to pick up on what they were doing well and initiate a positive contact home, or to pick up small misconceptions and errors (such as in spelling and punctuation).

There's no need to mark each book in detail, nor write anything at all. Just make a note to speak to that student about the work. You'll soon find that those students will start to make more progress.

Dot the SPaG

"Marking now takes me less time as the students are doing the work."

Save time picking out spelling mistakes for students by getting them to do all of the work. This simple idea will improve students' spelling, punctuation and grammar.

The secret to success in geography is to support and develop literacy development, especially the use of key geographical words and phrases. The trouble is that highlighting and correcting each error takes a very long time and if the same mistakes keep cropping up, it's not clear whether progress is being made. In addition, planning time is often compromised.

The small tweak to this is to put a small dot on the page if there is a mistake in the spelling, punctuation or grammar. This lets the student know that all is not right, and it is up to them to rectify the situation. Giving over five or ten minutes at the start of the lesson and expecting the class to find and correct the mistakes is likely to lead to fewer mistakes being made.

This idea can be developed further by getting the students to either peer- or self-assess their work before they hand it in. Ask them to place their exercise book into one of three piles: pile one if they are confident that there are no errors; pile two if they are unsure; pile three if they are not confident about their spelling. Keep this routine going and over time you'll see students' SPaG get better!

Teaching tip

Use the self-assessment piles to target your feedback conversations the following lesson to those that need additional support.

Target tracker

"Know where your students are!"

The trouble with progress is that it's very messy. Learning has ebbs and flows and students do better at some times than at others. By tracking their performance in assessments over time, it's much easier to get a clear picture of how they are doing over time.

Teaching tip

Graphs or tracking grids are great frames of reference in conversations with students in class and with parents. Don't let the grid be consigned to gather dust, use it regularly and refer to it often.

The best way to produce a target tracker is to get visual in the form of a graph or tracking grid. You also need to decide whether it will be made public, to instil a sense of competition, or private. Personally I stick them to the back cover of the students' exercise book or folder. Next decide on what you're tracking; this could be GCSE grades in the form of 9–1, A level grades, raw assessment marks or percentages. The important thing is to keep it consistent across all assessments. Mark the assessment scale on the vertical axis and leave lots of blanks on the horizontal axis to add the date in. You should have something that looks like this, only at A4 scale:

Grade

9

8

7

6

5

4

3

2

1

Date: 09.09   06.10   07.11   14.12   03.01   04.02   12.03   14.04

Bonus idea ★

In life after levels it's almost impossible to keep a clear idea of what's going on. Stick to something simple and give out a percentage or raw mark. Apply this consistently over every unit and a clear picture of progression will start to emerge.

Make it a part of your routine after every assessment point to ask students to add the date and shade in the box. You'll soon see a clear pattern emerge and students have a clear sense of progression, increasing their motivation.

Talk to them!

"Having a conversation with my teacher meant that I really understood what I needed to do to improve my work."

Teaching is hectic. As soon as the first morning bell goes we travel at 100 miles per hour and think we are expected to perform over and over. Slow down a little, set some time for some simpler consolidation activities and hold conversations with your students and they'll soon be producing brilliant work.

The trick here is to approach each unit as a sequence of work, split into various stages. There are a number of points when holding a conversation is worthwhile, e.g. in the run up to a major, high stakes assessment; just before a data entry point; toward the end of a unit.

By taking a holistic approach to the curriculum, it is perfectly acceptable to set some consolidation work for the class whilst you hold conversations with individual students. Examples of such work include: creating mind maps from exercise books or textbooks as revision, using the internet to follow a web enquiry or completing a past paper.

The aim is to chat to each student for a couple of minutes. I'd recommend sharing their target tracker (Idea 68) as well as flicking through their exercise book. It's also worth asking a few questions, e.g.

- What do you think your main strength is in geography?
- What can I help you with the most?
- Why is your homework always late?

The answers to these can throw up some issues that are simple to fix and it shows the students you care.

Finally, let them ask any questions that they may have. They'll leave the conversation feeling confident about what they need to improve.

Teaching tip

If you're not lucky enough to have double lessons or have a particularly large group, either hold the conversations over two or three lessons or set up a rolling programme in which you speak to a couple of students each lesson whilst the other students think and write.

Question level analysis

"Setting up the grids is worth it when the improvement is so measurable a couple of weeks later."

Reviewing exam papers is always tricky, so make the time more productive by getting the students to break down their performance by question.

Teaching tip

Whenever you conduct a test, even if it's a short one, insist on exam conditions and timed answers. This allows students to practise their exam technique and builds their confidence so that they can focus on the geography.

If you're like me, you set regular low stakes tests and exam practice so that the students get used to applying their geographical knowledge and understanding exam conditions. The more they practise, the better they will perform in the examination. Next time you feed back, take the time to conduct question level analysis. Firstly, create a simple grid to give to students, e.g.

Question No	Topic	Marks	My Score	Action to improve
1(a) (i) (ii) (iii)	Describing distribution	3		
1(a) (iv)	Comparing distribution	2		
1(a) (v)	Matching definitions	2		
1(a) (vi)	Explain why a site is suitable using map evidence	3		
1(b) (i)	Describe graph using data	2		
1(b) (ii)	Internet shopping – why it has expanded	2		
1(c) (i)	Using information to explain the effect on quality of life	4		
1(d)	Giving advantages and disadvantages for local people with new supermarket	4		
1(e)	Case study: Rocinha – rural to urban migration	5 + (3 QWC)		

Taking it further

If your classes are anything like mine, there will be some areas for which everyone can improve. In that case, it's easy to produce a sequence of lessons that tackles the gaps in their knowledge, therefore saving time going over topics that they are confident with.

Get the students to fill the rest of the grid in as they look over the paper. Don't worry too much about the overall grade, as it is more important to find out where the improvements can be made. At the end of the exercise, without having to go through each question with the whole class, each individual will be aware of where they could have improved. Their revision can then be directed towards that topic.

The most important step is then to repeat the low stakes test about two or three weeks later and measure the improvement by repeating the exercise.

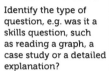

Bonus idea ★

Identify the type of question, e.g. was it a skills question, such as reading a graph, a case study or a detailed explanation?

Target sheets

"Without a doubt the biggest feedback timesaver ever!"

Save time and avoid the need to write the same thing over and over again by creating feedback sheets and marking codes.

Teaching tip

Differentiate the target sheets by placing a slightly different version in the exercise books of those who are high attainers. This sets the expectation that they should be working at a higher level.

Students want to know how to improve, so create a set of numbered target sheets. The first five or six targets can be generic, but the others can be adjusted to meet the year group and topic, e.g.

- Ensure that diagrams and handwriting are neat and legible.
- Use capital letters for place names such as the USA and Cardiff.
- Check spellings.
- Use the correct geographical terms.
- Don't use banned words.
- Use evidence from maps, photographs, data sources and articles.
- Give the opinions of at least two different groups of people with opposing views.
- Write about how places have changed over time.
- Link your answers to sustainable development.
- Give conclusions and make recommendations based on your evidence.

Stick the target sheet in the front of student exercise books and match them to assessment criteria and mark schemes. You will save yourself time that can be redirected into planning the next lessons by writing simply the number relating to what the student has either done well or needs to improve on, instead of the whole sentence. During a feedback session, students can then check your marking against the target sheet and understand what they need to work on.

Bonus idea ★

Get the students to hand in their exercise books open at the work you wish to mark. You'll be surprised at how much time is saved for each set of books.

Pupils are humans

"Great outcomes are built on positive relationships."

Although the education system is highly accountable, we still teach individuals; pupils are humans before they are ever statistics and intervention groups. Getting to know your students will help build excellent relationships upon which fantastic progress can be made.

One of the first things I do with every class is to ask them to write a couple of lines in their exercise books about themselves based on the following questions:

- What do you expect from geography this year?
- What do you expect from yourself?
- What do you expect from me?
- What is one thing I should know about you?

This activity provides a wealth of information that will help you to establish positive relationships with each individual student. Taking some time after the first lesson to read and respond to the students' writing will equip you with information to use during the next meet and greet (Idea 44) or other conversation with them.

Couple this information with your seating plan, an often-underused resource. The seating plan is essentially a map of your class that helps you know the individuals. It should include: their name; prior attainment; pupil premium (PP) or SEND; interests and current level of progress compared to their target.

Seating plans can also be used to create a heat map of your teaching. Ask a student to volunteer to mark your interactions on the seating plan. Who do you ask questions to and where do you walk and stand to give instructions? This information can feed into your lesson reflections, allowing small tweaks.

Taking it further

Make sure that every student that comes into your room has human contact by shaking their hand as you greet them. In addition, make sure you speak to every one at some point in the lesson, even if it is only when looking over their shoulder to point out a spelling mistake.

Bonus idea ★

Speed up report writing by getting the students to write their own just before the data entry deadline. Also ask them to provide some comments on your own performance; you'll be surprised at their candour, and the information can help tweak your teaching and identify areas of strength, which is great for appraisal time.

Keep expectations high

"My teacher expects a lot from me, but I rise to the challenge."

Large parts of a child's secondary school journey can lack challenge, especially when compared to the primary years. Combat what can be the lost years of education by always setting the bar high and maintaining your expectations. Students will rise to and enjoy the challenge.

Teaching tip

High expectations don't happen by accident. Make sure that you sit down with your department teammates and identify then agree the aspects of all lessons.

There are five ways in which teachers can set high expectations for their classes:

1. Provide high-quality teaching and learning from lesson one of Year 7.

Piling in the interventions in later years doesn't work as well as setting a culture of high expectations from lesson one of Year 7. Set extended writing challenges, insist on working in silence from time to time and never ever simplify the language; use the correct terminology from the word go. Sweat the small things such as spelling and presentation. Don't teach map skills; give students maps and expect them to interpret them.

2. Include exam questions as part of every lesson

This is not the same as becoming an exam factory, but every lesson should use the terminology and command words encountered at GCSE and A level. This forms powerful learning habits and a deeper understanding of questioning. There was a trend toward longer assessments and no exams in KS3, but all year groups should encounter exams and tests often.

3. Use the GCSE specification to inform KS3

Yes, there are topics that we need to cover, however KS3 should build up to later years so introducing some A level ideas and concepts is never a bad thing. Don't accept banned words (Idea 18) ever, and introduce Social, Economic, Environmental and Political straight away.

4. Teach a curriculum driven by enquiry

Fill your curriculum full of JONK: the Joy Of Not Knowing and communicate that it's OK to find topics difficult and to not always know the answers. Instead, use the enquiry process to help students work their way out of it. After all, if we only every taught the stuff we know the answer to, what's the point in learning?

5. Develop the mantras of 'So what?' and 'Prove it!' (Idea 23)

Expect your students to expand their answers wherever answers can be expanded further, answering the question, 'So what?'. Prompt them to include evidence after every geographical point made, in response to the instruction, 'Prove it!'.

Geography gems

"When I was stuck I could fall back on the geography gems."

Students have to deal with many examinations. Make their life a little more bearable by continually reinforcing the geography gems and, when panic sets in, they will fall back upon them.

Teaching tip

Geography Gems are only as good as the number of times you refer to them. Ensure that they are embedded in schemes of work and that students have plenty of opportunities to practice using them. Consider putting them up in a display so that you can easily refer to them when teaching.

Quality geography is about being able to communicate an argument in a concise, precise manner. Students also have to replicate this under exam conditions whilst trying to remember the case study facts. Ease the pressure a little by teaching these golden geographical gems, which can easily be applied to a wide range of questions.

- The elderly and very young tend to lose out. Whether it's a heat wave, the local post office closing or a tropical storm, these groups of people are less resilient to change.
- Improving the lives of women in developed countries means that their time can be spent being economically active, earning extra income. Extra income in a community means that more tax revenue is available for investment, therefore community infrastructure can be improved.
- Poorer countries are unable to plan, prepare and predict for disasters as the infrastructure is poor and there is a lack of capital for prevention techniques. This goes for flood and coastal defences too, where the priority is given to basic social needs such as health and education.
- Poor sanitation results in preventable diseases which stop people working.
- Ease of access to transport infrastructure for goods, employees and consumers means that shopping centres, industry and the central business district (CBD) are relocated.

#geoggem

- Land is cheaper when it is less desirable, e.g. on flood plains or in shanty towns and industrial areas.
- Multiplier effect: the positive and negative multiplier effect links to many economic questions and migration.
- Deforestation and urbanisation are bad as they increase the risk of flooding, reduce biodiversity and release carbon dioxide.
- People generally hate ugly things such as sea defences.

Furnished with these golden arguments, students are able to structure an answer for a wide range of questions if their mind goes blank in the examination hall. The golden arguments are also peppered with key geographical terms so revisit them often and display them in your classroom. They won't cover every eventuality, but keeping a focused list is good.

It's also worth adding a list of arguments that should never be used, e.g. their quality of life gets better; it's economically sustainable; the country gets richer...

Taking it further

Don't constrain this idea to exam classes: instead, set it free in the lower school. By making younger students aware of some core geographical gems, they will be able to practise using them and will be more likely to remember them when it comes to exam time.

Decision structure

"This structure helped my students get the best marks in the decision-making paper."

Decision-making exercises are a geography staple but can be bewildering to students. Giving them this structure will not only improve their answers but also build their confidence in tackling large essays in examinations.

Teaching tip

Use this idea together with Idea 20 (V.C.O.G) to build the confidence of lower attainers before slowly removing the extra help as the quality of their answers improves.

The decision-making examination paper is an opportunity for students to apply their geographical knowledge to an unknown scenario, which is what quality geography is all about. Follow this structure, modified for your particular examination board and their confidence will grow.

The first thing is to get the students to glance at the choices contained in the question. Although this is usually the last question, the whole paper usually builds towards the decision. Therefore, being aware of the choice right from the start helps students. Encourage them to create a quick planning grid like the one below in which they can add information as they go along.

	Positive	Negative
Option 1		
Option 2		
Option 3		

Their notes should be short, containing the resource reference and name of the stakeholders involved. Done well, this will form their plan for the final essay question.

Most decision-making exercises are in essay form and carry a lot of marks. Give the following structure to your classes and they will soon learn it, freeing up their thinking time for the application of geographical knowledge and extended arguments.

- Start with your conclusion in a sentence.
- Give two well-developed points that outline the advantages of your choice.
- Give one well-developed point about the disadvantage of your scheme.
- Give at least two simple advantages and disadvantages of every other scheme. Link them to your choice if possible.
- Link your work to a global issue such as climate change, migration, economic development or sea level change.
- End with your conclusion.

Ensure that students understand that decision-making papers contain a wealth of information for them to use, however they must do something with it: simply copying out the information will lose marks. Using 'this means that' and 'so' connectives (Idea 26) helps with this.

Introduce this structure early on, stick to it and ensure that your entire curriculum contains opportunities to write decision-making essays at regular intervals and you'll soon find that the quality of geographical writing improves.

Homework as the lesson

"I've lost count of the times this has saved me in admin time."

Homework is a marmite subject for geography teachers and one where you're damned if you do or if you don't. Simply, set homework that builds into, and is used within, the next lesson and see your workload reduce.

Teaching tip

Most schools have a way of contacting home via text message, use this to remind students' parents that homework is due and include a hyperlink to some online help sheets or activities.

As a younger teacher, I spent an inordinate amount of time chasing homework that wasn't completed, setting detentions and contacting home. Inspiration came, of all places, from the Ofsted teaching and learning criteria where it was mentioned that homework should form an integral part of the lesson. The term 'flipped learning' has become popular lately, but it's just good practice.

It's simple really, set homework that is used in the lesson, e.g.

- Set a homework that will ensure that a class have revised continents and oceans before a sequence of lessons on tectonic plates.
- Set an exam question that will be peer-marked in class.
- Get students to complete a survey at home that will be used in class to develop data handling skills.
- Practise grid reference and map symbol skills before lessons on land use.

There are many benefits to this. Firstly, those students who haven't done the homework will become obvious to you and will feel the pressure to conform as they will see the point of the homework. Secondly, your time spent marking homework will diminish as you'll soon find that the proportion of students not doing homework falls, meaning less time chasing and contacting home for negative reasons.

Handing in books open

"Genius!"

Marking and feedback are essential activities but doing it right is time-consuming. This simple hack will save a surprising amount of time, allowing you to focus on the feedback and not the faff.

While visiting a feeder primary school, I noticed that there was a pile of books in the corner that were all open. When I enquired about this the teacher explained that getting the pupils to hand in books open at the work that needed to be marked saved time. I needed to try this for myself so, on return to my class, I asked a group to hand in the work open at the page that I wanted to mark.

This very simple tweak to routine saves a surprising amount of time and will allow you to focus on the geography and marking rather than finding the appropriate work.

Taking it further

Combine this idea with asking students to peer-assess each other's work for spelling, punctuation and grammatical errors. They should then correct them before handing in their work, saving even more time.

Quick wins

Part 7

Would you rather

"Blimey! That got me thinking!"

Starting lessons with a really tricky dilemma is great for getting students to think hard as well as consolidating knowledge and improving long-term memory of important topics.

Teaching tip

Although 'Would you rather' works well when exploring your current topic, its effects are even better when thrown in at the start or end of a lesson on a different topic. This places a demand on students to recall information, helping them to embed it into their long-term memory.

Recent research suggests that revisiting topics often, or interleaving, is a great way to aid students in remembering the knowledge required to do well in examinations. After visiting the classroom of Leah Sharp, a primary teacher in Sussex, I often start lessons with a geographical 'Would you rather' question.

For example, when developing case study exam technique, I ask students would they rather write an answer full of facts or an answer with two facts that is well developed. The discussion develops their understanding of what good geography is as well as familiarising them with the mark scheme. In this case, it's important to give well-developed answers based around a few place-specific facts. The impact is that students focus their revision on the facts that link together and that they can develop well.

Try these examples. Would you rather:

- live in a rich or poor country susceptible to earthquakes?
- be lost in the desert or lost in the tropical rainforest?
- migrate from an urban area or to an urban area?
- eat locally-sourced produce or eat what you want when you want it?
- include a small amount of quantitative data or a large amount of qualitative?

Boom! Such dilemmas get students really thinking about wider geographical issues as well as exam technique.

Decision dice

"Using the decision dice, I found writing so much easier."

Often the biggest hurdle is getting students to start writing about an idea. Others stumble to a halt after getting down their number one idea and then struggle to add another. This idea provides a stimulus for students without giving too much support.

Every so often, I want students to be independent with their writing without the crutch of a writing frame or other scaffold. The problem is that they can become too reliant on never having to think about the next step. In addition, at some point in their future there will be an exam or test that provides minimal structure. This idea is easy to set up but very effective.

Start by setting the task, e.g. 'How is conflict managed between different users of Dawlish Warren?' Provide minimal support and encourage the students to write as independently as possible, but give them a 2 x 3 grid filled with ideas, e.g.

When stuck, students simply roll a dice, look at the corresponding square then think about how the word or phrase links to the answer. Students often start to remember the information taught previously and the element of randomness keeps them on their toes.

Although the dice provides a little randomness, ensure that you insist on a decent piece of writing being produced!

Teaching tip

Dice are fantastic, but invest in some of the foam silent ones so you won't have to live with the clattering.

Taking it further

It's possible to vary the grids by:
creating up to 12 squares; either providing two dice or rolling twice and adding up the score.
Including dates, facts and information or pictorial evidence.
Providing a little more information in each square.

Storm audio

"I'll never forget hearing that forecast!"

Audio clips are brilliant in geography. The National Hurricane Centre (NHC) in the USA provides advisory information in the form of maps, text and graphs but it also provides brief podcasts that allow students to appreciate the danger faced.

Teaching tip

Listen to the audio clip first, but also make use of the excellent maps, graphs and other information provided by the NHC. In addition, after listening to the clip, ask students to write a description of what they expect the place to look like after the storm. Then show the images of the aftermath.

Taking it further

Record your own podcasts about case studies, key ideas and other geographical units. Short three–four minute clips are easy to create and publish using mobile devices and freely available apps.

Head along to the NHC's podcast page: www. nhc.noaa.gov/audio. There you'll find any current advisories. Be warned, they only display the most current one and if there is no current tropical storm activity you'll need to navigate to the archive. This podcast made during Hurricane Sandy is a good example to use, and is still relevant today: www.nhc.noaa.gov/audio/archive/201210300003.mp3.

Play the podcast three times. The first time just ask students to listen to the information. What leaps out at them? How would they feel as a resident or business owner hearing that advisory? The second time, get pupils to identify and write down key information such as the height of the storm surge or speed of the wind. During the third airing, get them to pick up any additional information that they may have missed.

Next, use the classroom environment to put the numbers into context, e.g. how high is the storm surge compared to the classroom? This technique often brings home the power of tropical storms and your classes will develop empathy with the residents.

Where my stuff comes from

"I never knew that I was connected to so many places!"

Globalisation means that the average student is connected to many different countries through the clothes they wear and things they use during the day. This activity links them personally as consumers to other places around the world.

This idea works as a great homework mapping activity before following up in the classroom. It can include anything or be limited, e.g. food or sports clothing. Give students the following table and ask them to add to it by looking for labels at home. Make sure you get students to look at at least fifty items so that they are able to spot the patterns.

Teaching tip

I'd recommend having a completed table that you've done yourself, for students that were absent when the homework was set.

Item	Country of origin/ manufacture	Company or brand	Location of brand HQ
iPhone	China	Apple	USA, Dublin
Xbox controller	China	Microsoft	USA, UK
Fleece/jacket	Cambodia	Mountain Equipment	UK

Once the information is collected, it can be looked at in many ways, e.g.

- What type of country are their possessions manufactured in? What is their GDP and how do they compare with the UK?
- Where are the brand HQs located? What type of country are they?
- Is there a difference between where clothes are manufactured compared to electronics?
- How many things come through the piracy hotspots, the Gulf of Aden or South China Sea?

Create graphs and choropleth maps from the data and discuss the most appropriate type of graph for each.

Taking it further

As multinational companies strive to be open and transparent, many of them are putting their supply chains on the internet. Search the websites of major companies and map where the individual components of items come from. The airbus A380 is a great example!

Matching stats to images

"And I thought I really knew the city I've lived in for 15 years!"

The internet is a wonderful place and now enables census information to be found quickly. This activity will challenge the misconceptions that your students have of their local area.

Teaching tip

As with many aspects of geography, knowing the definitions is vital so spend some time ensuring that each class understands the meaning of each variable.

This idea requires a bit of preparation, but it is worth doing as students will gain a deeper understanding of their local area and of the information contained within the census. First, select around five local wards from the nearest urban area. Either visit each location and take a photograph, or use Google Street View to grab a screenshot. The photos form the first part of the resource.

Next, visit the neighbourhood statistics website: www.neighbourhood.statistics.gov.uk. The site visualises the census data down to ward level. There is an almost infinite amount of data. Choose around four variables and create a table of the corresponding information, e.g.

Name of ward (and photo)	Number of full-time students	Number of graduates	Deprivation index	Housing tenure	Homelessness
A					
B					

Cut the table into individual cards and ask the class to match each card to the correct place. Students will quickly develop the ability to link different variables together and will hypothesise about various causes. You'll also find out how much they don't know about their local area!

GaugeMap

"Real time tweeting river gauges!"

Using GaugeMap is simple and effective and will improve your students' understanding of the complex relationship between precipitation and river flow.

In an ideal world, rain would fall and then we would take our class out to sit on the riverbank, timing how long it took for the water to get in to the river. That's not possible, but GaugeMap is the next best thing (www.gaugemap.co.uk). It is an interactive map that lists thousands of flow gauges around the country. And it's in real time! Selecting a location displays a graph showing the river's discharge over the last few days.

Ensure that you have covered the main parts of the hydrological cycle and flood hydrographs first, then use GaugeMap to help consolidate existing knowledge, e.g.

- Filter stations for those that are at risk of flooding or below their usual range. Look for patterns by comparing the locations with recent weather and climate maps available from the Met Office.
- Show a coastal location graph and ask students to explain the daily increases in discharge (tides).
- Search for your local river. Where are the stations located? Is there a reason for this? E.g. some stations are placed upstream of major settlements or transport infrastructure.
- If you are planning a fieldtrip to a river, check it out on GaugeMap first. Where are the stations? What are the characteristics of its flow? What is the river basin like?
- If a river is in flood, how does it compare to the record flow marked on the graph.

Teaching tip

Many of the stations have their own Twitter feed so it's worth following a few relevant ones, especially when heavy or prolonged precipitation is expected.

Taking it further

If a major flood event happens in the holidays, or indeed at any time, use GaugeMap to explore the affected rivers. Collect a bank of screenshots and ask the students to arrange them into chronological order.

Bonus idea ★

When teaching floating topicality, visit a river on GaugeMap after a major rainfall event to watch its response. Does it flood? Do two rivers in the same area react the same or differently? How long does it take for the river's discharge to rise afterwards? Take screenshots to build up a visual record.

Globalisation YouTube quiz

"A simple idea that is easily adapted."

YouTube is a great resource. This idea harnesses the power of advertising to hammer home the point that the world's multinational companies operate in many diverse environments whilst looking remarkably similar!

Teaching tip

It's really useful to be able to freeze the screen or, using the old-fashioned method, hold a book in front of the lens when opening up each clip so the students aren't able to spot the name of the clip before you are able to get it full screen.

I love YouTube. It's taught me how to repair a tent, put up shelves and build some awesome creations in Minecraft that beat my son's! However, this idea is linked with adverts. I wanted to show students that multinational giants like Coca-Cola and McDonald's get into almost every culture in the world and yet look the same and are identifiable.

In advance of the lesson, search on YouTube for McDonald's and Coca-Cola adverts from different parts of the world and paste the hyperlinks into PowerPoint. In the lesson, play each clip with the sound down and ask the class to guess its location. Revisit each clip after they have guessed the answer and discuss which ones they found surprising.

Students can also identify the common branding and deepen their understanding of globalisation. The beauty of using McDonald's, which is familiar to most students, is that they will also start to spot glocalisation – where products have been altered to fit in with local customs and culture.

MEDC or not?

"Sir really challenges my thinking!"

This simple idea challenges individuals' misconceptions about parts of the world and the importance of reliable data. It's easily adapted too, so the applications are almost endless!

One powerful misconception that students often have is to think that photographs are representative of an area when in fact other information is always needed, e.g. they might think that it is possible to identify the development level of a country by a photograph alone.

Teaching tip

Don't use this activity too often though, as the students soon catch on!

Create ten slides in PowerPoint with an image on each one of a different location in the world. Mix up the more economically developed and less economically developed countries (MEDCs and LEDCs), and choose photographs that are not representative of the country, e.g. a photograph of Sao Paulo's CBD; an exotic beach in Cuba; the lions in Longleat.

Simply display each image and ask individuals to decide whether the country is most likely to be a rich or poor country, citing reasons for their choice. Of course, the answers are likely to be opposite of what they think, hammering home that development data is required to be sure. This lesson can then move into different indicators of development.

The idea can be adapted to cover many aspects of geography, e.g.

- Cardiff or not? Take images around your local area to see if students can identify their locality.
- Urban or rural? Mix images of urban parks with countryside locations.
- Physical or human geography?

Students will develop their classification skills using this activity.

Sustainability pledge

"Changing your lifestyle is really difficult!"

Sometimes the trouble with geography is that it becomes theoretical and based on other people's opinions and experiences who are often removed from the school environment. By challenging your students to make a change at home, they will appreciate just how difficult it is to change the world!

Teaching tip

Make sure you embed homework into your schemes of work so that the activities allow students to extend skills; practice knowledge recall and see geography in action all around them. Remember, the appeal of our subject is that it can be experienced, measured and observed in the real world that our young people inhabit.

Taking it further

Once your class have experienced what it is like to change a small aspect of their lives, set up a sustainability club in school and set them the challenge of reducing the environmental impact of your institution. They can use their personal experience to inform their planning and think about how they will inform others.

Teaching about climate change and sustainability is embedded into geography departments these days and I often see the concept of ecological footprints being taught. Go one step further than asking students to calculate their carbon footprint by challenging them to change one aspect of their lifestyle, e.g. can they convince their entire family to switch to showers or to walk to the shop instead of taking a five-minute drive, or not to leave the television on standby?

Once each individual identifies a change they can make, ask them to make a pledge by committing it to paper and displaying it in your classroom. Next, get each student to keep a diary and give them a decent timescale, ideally a month.

At the end of the month, compare stories. How many students have been able to make a change? What were the barriers or support that they had? What did other people think of the change?

By carrying out this mini project, students will gain a greater insight into why carbon offsetting and trading are attractive prospects for large companies and organisations. They'll also understand how difficult it is for a whole country to reduce their emissions!

Spot the border!

"A great activity to develop satellite interpretation skills."

Human activity makes its mark on the Earth's surface and one place that this can be illustrated is at border crossings. This idea allows students to appreciate the impact that imaginary lines have on the physical environment.

The Earth is criss-crossed with imaginary lines. Some mark out lines of latitude and longitude whilst others mark out the international boundaries between nations. Ask the students a simple question: 'What will the border between country x and country y look like?' Great examples can be found between the USA and its neighbours Mexico and Canada, although any land border in the world is well worth examination.

Next, fire up Google Earth, ensuring that all of the layers are switched off so no words are visible on the map. Then:

- Navigate to near the border and ask students to work out where the actual border is using clues in the physical and human geography of the area.
- Ask students to be brave and come up to the board and draw on where they think the border is. Get them to justify their decision based upon the geography.
- Reveal the location of the border by selecting the 'Borders and places' layer. Compare their lines to the real imaginary border.
- Finish the activity by asking students to list the impacts that imaginary borders have on the human and physical geography of the area.

This idea gets students to think about the impact of borders as well as developing their satellite interpretation skills and reinforcing the difference between physical and human geography.

Taking it further

Get the class to compare two different borders of the same country, e.g. how does the USA's border with Canada compare to the one with Mexico? Why are there any differences? Use internet research to supplement this, especially where borders have caused conflict such as between India and Pakistan.

Keeping geography dynamic

Part 8

Living curriculum

"Planning was made so much easier as we all had access to the same resources and ideas."

Although teachers are great magpies, sometimes we don't share as much as we should within our department. As a result, what is taught often varies between members of the same team. Cloud computing now makes shared schemes of work that are accessible to everyone.

Taking it further

Use a cloud service for all of your department's needs: meeting minutes, tracking documents, fieldwork booking forms, etc.

The fundamental building block of a top quality geography curriculum is the scheme of work, because success comes from great sequences of lessons, not a one-off performance. Great schemes of work ensure that students get exposed to the same opportunities and members of staff become more confident as they are able to cover the precise information required by the exam board. Make your schemes of work accessible and collaborative by using a cloud service such as Google Docs. Create a document and share it with all of your colleagues.

By making the document accessible to all, it becomes 'living' and teachers can link to new resources and ideas. Couple this idea with a Dropbox subscription or use a free cloud service such as Office365 or Google Docs, and your team will be able to access everything within one simple document.

Over time, you'll find your workload decreasing and that the sequences of lessons in your department match the dynamic nature of our subject. Furthermore, by keeping schemes of work online, they won't become fossilised documents and will ensure that teachers can focus on planning for every pupil instead of reinventing the wheel.

Google Alerts

"My lessons use far more current events and ideas now than they ever did before."

Our wonderful subject benefits from being linked to the world outside as it happens now. Using Google Alerts will ensure you keep up to date so there is no danger of passing out of date information to the students, whether it's about that local planning issue or an international relief effort.

Google Alerts is a free, easy-to-use web service found at www.google.co.uk/alerts.

Essentially, the user writes a search term, as you would when looking for information on the internet, and saves it. Then, Google Alerts will email the information in a handy format. This allows busy teachers to keep up-to-date with events, and you'll soon find videos, news stories and resources sailing into your inbox. Currently, my alerts are:

- Iceland tectonic activity volcano
- i360 Brighton
- OCR B geography GCSE
- Ebola
- UK flooding
- pupil premium
- HS2
- Calais the 'Jungle' refugees.

Using Google Alerts is a huge time-saver and will ensure that your lessons are dynamic and up-to-date.

Teaching tip

Make sure that you choose the weekly email option and limit yourself to half a dozen alerts, otherwise your inbox will start overflowing, which is very counterproductive!

Spot the headline!

"This activity challenged my misconceptions and stereotypes."

One of the most fascinating aspects of geography teaching is covering controversial topics such as migration, and it is our duty to ensure that students leave us with an understanding of the complexity of such high profile events.

Teaching tip

Follow the headlines with some hard data. The Office for National Statistics, for example, has fantastic data on international migration. This gives an opportunity to develop those important maths skills at the same time.

This idea challenges students' preconceptions and/or misconceptions in a non-threatening way.

Display a headline and a few extracts from a suitable news story and related questions, and set up a PowerPoint slide to slowly reveal them, e.g.

- 'Astounding new figures show record numbers of migrants are crossing the world in search of better lifestyles.'
- Should they be welcomed?
- Are they a burden?
- Should they go back to where they came from?

It's likely that students would assume that the article is referring to migrants into the UK when in fact the news story is all about British expats heading to the sunny shores of the Mediterranean. Ask the class to predict what the headline is referring to, to ask questions and identify what further information they need.

After revealing the truth, allow the students to read the full article and identify the pull and push factors before moving on to consider migrations into the UK. You'll soon find that students become more open to controversial ideas.

Newspaper talking heads

"Before, I used to rack my brain in order to provide different points of view; now it's quick and easy."

One of the most difficult aspects of geography for students to get to grips with is being able to appreciate different points of view. With the advent of online newspapers, it has never been easier to gather these views, especially on local issues.

I often used to spend many, many hours putting together talking head style resources to furnish my classes with different points of view. Textbooks often do this for us, but not consistently enough, and perhaps not on local issues, which are more relevant to the school's context. Whilst much journalism is often a bit dubious, the great British public really like commenting online on news stories.

Simply head to a newspaper and search for a news story. A great example is the i360 tower that can be found in Brighton: the local newspaper is always full of stories about it and the issue divides opinion in the local area.

Next, skim over the actual article and head to the comments below it. You'll find these to be a lively hotbed of debate and opinion. Cherry-pick the best comments that represent different points of view and voila! You have some talking heads that provide authentic different opinions on the local ideas.

This idea saves planning time and makes case studies more memorable.

Teaching tip

I wouldn't recommend asking students to directly access the content as conversations can become feral, even with good moderation procedures in place. Students will also spend a lot of time reading comments instead of understanding their context.

Blind drawing

"This helped me to remember the key points of each diagram."

Geography is full of diagrams and sketches, and these can help students retain information as well as improve their written work. This simple idea pairs up students so that they can develop their drawing skills.

Taking it further

This idea is easily adapted to cover a range of diagrams, e.g. types of rainfall, erosion processes, weather and climate.

By way of an example for this idea, I am using the concept of constructive and destructive waves, although it is easily adaptable to other concepts. It works best when encountering an unknown concept that hasn't been taught yet.

- Get students in pairs.
- Issue each pair with a mini whiteboard and a pen.
- Each pair needs to have one person with their back to the board while the other faces it.
- Reveal the diagram on the board.
- The student with their back to the board must draw the diagram without looking at it, using the directions, descriptions and ideas from their partner who can see the diagram.
- Swap roles and reveal a different diagram, in this case the other type of wave.

This activity works on improving accurate description skills as well as helping students remember the key diagram. Follow this up by challenging the students to draw at least one of the diagrams from memory into their exercise book, complete with accurate terminology.

You'll find that, when they are asked to reproduce the diagram weeks later, they are able to recall much more information than if they simply copied the diagram from a book or the board.

Think, pair, write, share

"Slowing the lesson down enabled every student to get involved."

In our rush to move on, there is often very little time for students to think about a question. Embed this simple idea into your teaching and you'll soon have all students thinking hard.

One of my mantras as a teacher is that we should encourage students to be 'stuck'. The problem with this is that we are often so worried about getting through the content that we don't allow students to be stuck for long, quickly rattling through question and answer sessions. Remember that some of the best teachers slow down. Using the 'think, pair, write, share' idea can help.

After posing a question, ask students to follow this sequence.

- **Think** for at least a minute – think means in silence without talking to anyone else. Don't even let the students write anything down at this point and use a timer to keep to the minute. No one should be talking, including yourself.
- **Pair** – the students share ideas with the person next to them. Were they thinking the same thing? Can the other person add anything to their thoughts and ideas.
- **Write** – at this point, get every individual to write a response in silence. This time allows the teacher to visit target students or those that may need a little boost.
- **Share** – students share their ideas in groups of four. Encourage students to modify their response here, by reading each other's ideas and work. Finally, select some students to share their ideas with the class.

Teaching tip

Use the writing time to look over students' work in the class. Then choose a shy student that you know has written a great answer to be the one to share their ideas with the class. For those that are extra shy, consider reading their work out for them or showing it via a visualiser.

Bonus idea

When communicating instructions or explanations to your students, choose one part of the room to stand in and stick to it and don't move around. This may be at the front of the class, at each of the cardinal compass points or another variation. This quickly becomes a silent cue that you will be expecting the class to listen.

Living continuum

"This ensured that I didn't sit on the fence and had a clear opinion instead."

Many concepts in geography are difficult to understand as they are quite abstract and theoretical. Also, for many topics there often isn't a 'correct' answer. By getting students out of their seats and sharing their viewpoints, they are able to justify their opinions as there's nowhere to hide.

Taking it further

Use the continuum to set different homework exercises, e.g. those that disagree should research the agree point of view and vice versa.

This idea needs nothing more than a couple of pieces of paper stuck to the wall at different ends of the classroom. The terms on the paper can range from 'agree' and 'disagree' to written concepts such as 'sustainable', 'exploitation' and 'conservation.' You can then create a continuum by displaying some questions for the students to think about, and asking each individual to decide where on the continuum they will stand.

For example, when exploring sustainable development, place 'conservation' and 'exploitation' at opposite ends of the room and 'sustainable development' in the middle. Show an image of gold mining in the Amazon or palm oil monoculture in Borneo. Ask students to decide their position along the continuum and move to it, then ask a few individuals to explain their choice.

The 'agree' vs 'disagree' line has many applications and it is worth keeping these permanently displayed at opposite ends of your classroom, e.g.

- The government response to Hurricane Katrina was effective.
- The 2010 eruption of Eyjafjallajökull affected Icelanders less than people living elsewhere.
- Trump should build a wall to stop illegal migration between Mexico and the USA.

This idea is fantastic for recapping case studies and exploring your students' viewpoints. Their understanding of complex concepts will also quickly improve.

Stereotype mapping

"Find out how well your class really knows the UK."

People think of places in different ways. In addition, some people know more about certain places than others. This idea can be used at a range of scales and explores students' existing ideas and stereotypes, although focusing on the UK will support students in tackling the increased focus on our home countries in the new GCSE specifications.

I was browsing the gapingvoid website (www. gapingvoid.com) one day when I came across a map of the USA divided by stereotypes and simple statements like 'flat', 'boring', 'the best', etc. It struck me that I didn't really know how much my students knew about the UK, the world or even their local area.

Get a blank map of the area that you wish to explore; I'd recommend starting with a map of the UK. Ask students to silently write and draw areas on their map, labelling their views of each place, e.g.

- 'Everyone wears kilts in Scotland.'
- 'Wales is full of sheep.'
- 'London is busy and frightening.'

There are a couple of skills in development here, as students can use an atlas to locate areas or do so from memory.

You can use the maps in a number of ways, e.g.

- Fill in the knowledge gaps about crucial places in terms of UK geography.
- Ask, 'Where does "the north" start? Is there data to support this?'
- Provide a list of the key human and physical features of the UK and ask the students to place them on the map.

Teaching tip

High-quality, free downloadable maps of the UK and the world are available on the Ordnance Survey website (www. ordnancesurvey.co.uk).

113

Ban paper and pens

"I really had to think how to communicate my idea to others."

Writing, literacy and numeracy are vital to geographers, but so is problem solving and creativity. Every now and again, it is worth limiting the resources available to students so that they have to think harder.

Teaching tip

This idea only works within a clearly defined learning outcome that is linked to some core geographical knowledge. For example, you may wish the class to demonstrate their knowledge of a particular case study or concept.

This is a great idea to use at a fieldwork location or onsite as a piece of doorstep geography. Ask the students to think of a favourite place. They should choose one that has both human and physical features. Next, set them a task with a clearly defined outcome, e.g. to describe the location of the place in relation to the school and communicate at least three human and three physical features of their chosen place. The rule is, they aren't allowed to use paper or pens, and certainly no clipboards.

Allow the students time to think a little and mind map ideas. This is problem solving at its best. The types of ideas that I have seen develop are:

- Short performances or drama pieces about their place.
- Students using the notepad function of their phones to make a list of bullet points before using them to read a news report.
- Creating maps from objects that are found around the classroom or school grounds.

This idea engages students in describing places and sharing ideas as well as encouraging problem-solving skills.

Mindfulness moment

"Breaking up a double lesson like this helped me to stay focused for the rest of the day."

Students get lots of lectures about trying their best and preparing for examinations. By modelling how to relax and by creating a little bit of time within your lessons, you'll help students tackle the pressures of school that little bit better.

I've always been a fan of stopping and looking; taking the time to notice the little things around me and taking a moment to savour the moment before continuing the journey forward. I first tried this idea in my double lessons to break up the two hours without allowing students out of the classroom to become distracted.

Simply, ask the class to put their pens down and sit comfortably. Get them to close their eyes and focus on their breathing, taking the time to take long breaths in and out, noticing their own rhythms and blocking out external sounds.

Set a timer for three minutes and just let the students sit and breathe. Model it yourself and soon your class will meet your expectation, although some will find it odd at first! After the three minutes are up, gently ask the class to open their eyes and get ready to move on.

You'll find that concentration improves and, as the rest button has effectively been pushed, they will be more open to a change of direction. This is an idea that they themselves can try before examinations and it models how to manage workload well.

Taking it further

Try this idea when out on fieldwork or teaching the variables of weather, but this time ask the students to notice what is around them rather than their own breathing. What do they hear and feel?

Teach using cake

"The introduction of cake into a lesson is always welcome!"

Although GIS packages help students understand the role that the underlying geology of an area has in shaping distinctive landforms, sometimes they need further visual confirmation of this. Additionally, it may not be possible to get out into the field to see the role of geology in person, so this idea uses layered cake to demonstrate how geology shapes our coastline.

Taking it further

Once students are familiar with the concept that the cake layers represent the different rock layers, get them to design a demonstration that describes the formation of other features such as waterfalls.

I came across this idea on the blog of Tony Cassidy, an inspirational and creative geographer. I've since used it year after year and find that students are able to remember the formation of various coastal and fluvial features much more easily than when drawing diagrams alone.

You'll need a cake that has three layers, like angel cake. These are easily found in most supermarkets and are relatively cheap. The different layers represent the variation in the geology of the underlying rock, e.g. when teaching the formation of a wave-cut platform and the process of cliff retreat, follow this demonstration:

- Remove a piece from the middle layer of the cake. This represents the wave-cut notch where the erosion process attacks the fault line.
- As the wave-cut notch gets deeper through continual erosion, gravity eventually causes the overhanging cliff (the top layer of the cake) to collapse. Remove the top layer and explain that wave action will transport the material away.
- The cliff position has retreated inland and the first layer of the cake represents the wave-cut platform.

This technique can be used to demonstrate other processes too, and you'll find that students are able to identify the landforms easily from photographs and maps as a result as well as remembering the sequence.

Giving students options

"The class were able to act as individuals and yet all demonstrated their knowledge of the process."

We often unintentionally restrict students by limiting their options. Whilst we have a duty to prepare them for examinations, having to transform information from one form to another helps them remember complex processes.

It's best to take a long-term view of this idea over a sequence of lessons joined by homework. Students should work individually or in pairs, anything larger than that and some will hide and do very little work. Once the teaching of the topic is over, set a question that will consolidate their knowledge.

For example, after looking at the Nepalese earthquake, ask students to describe the social, economic and environmental factors. Of course, we want students to be able to write a detailed response to this, however we help them remember by asking them to do something slightly different first. Give them a list of options, such as:

- a 'Dear John' letter from a climber explaining why he will never return to Everest again
- an RSA-style animation that explains the main economic, social and environmental impacts of the earthquake
- changing the lyrics of a well-known song to describe the devastation that occurred in Everest Base camp or Kathmandu
- a finger puppet news show that summarises the main chronology of the earthquake.

The idea is to provide a balanced mix of activities that will appeal to a wide range of learners to ensure that everyone gets involved as there are writing activities as well as more creative ideas.

You will find that the engagement of your class will increase and, when asked to write about the issue, their writing will improve. The bonus is that you also have a ready-made set of revision resources too!

Teaching tip

Set very clear success criteria and expectations of what needs to be covered and avoid activities that don't include words and writing.

117

Join a subject association

"It's good to know that I'm not alone."

The resources and support network available to teachers who are part of a subject association are second to none. Join one and reach out!

Taking it further

Both organisations have opportunities to volunteer and be involved in their work, from giving a talk at a conference to joining a committee. The upshot is that you will become better informed about crucial changes and updates, well before most other teachers. Therefore you'll be one step ahead!

Geography departments are usually small and therefore it can be difficult to build up a good support network locally – there are even one-person departments. The joining fee of both the Geographical Association (GA) and Royal Geographical Society (RGS) is worth it for so many reasons:

- CPD – both organisations offer journals and courses and have great websites that are full of teaching resources and ideas. The bonus is that they are all vetted and created by geographers, so you know they will be high quality. The RGS even provides a chartered geographer accreditation for those who have been in the profession for six years or more.
- TeachMeets – both organisations run geography-focused TeachMeets where ideas are shared in an informal atmosphere. Keep an eye on social media for details on how to get involved.
- The GA conference – the highlight of the geographical year. Three days packed with CPD for new teachers, primary geographers and subject updates as well as the traditional social gatherings and support networks.

You'll find yourself more informed, better supported and your enthusiasm invigorated!